The Art and Wonder of
Origami

Kunihiko Kasahara

This book features a CD-ROM with how-to Flash movies to help anyone understand the world of origami, including brain-stretching puzzles, traditional forms,
three-dimensional models, and stunningly beautiful works of art.

t designs are provided on the CD-ROM.

The Art and Wonder of Origami
© 2004 by Kunihiko Kasahara

First published in 2004 in Japan by
Gijutsu Hyoron-sha Publishing Co., Ltd.
under the title of *Jiturei mansai! Koko made dekiru origami no miryoku to fushigi*

First published in the United States of America by
Quarry Books, a member of
Quayside Publishing Group
33 Commercial Street
Gloucester, Massachusetts 01930-5089
Telephone: (978) 282-9590
Fax: (978) 283-2742
www.rockpub.com

with the rights and production arrangements of
Rico Komanoya, ricorico, Tokyo Japan

Translation: Tom Boatman, Minoru Okajima, and Minako Sakagami (native creative Y.K.)
Art direction and book design: Eiko Nishida (cooltiger)
CD-ROM authoring and manufacturing: TimezProShop
Chief editor and producer: Rico Komanoya (ricorico)

ISBN 1-59253-213-6
10 9 8 7 6 5 4 2 1

Printed in Singapore

Foreword

How Old Is Origami?

For more than 300 years, origami techniques have been passed down in Japan from mother to child, and the tradition continues today.

But origami's true origins probably date back even further. What we call *paper* was invented in China 2,000 years ago. More than 2,000 years before that, papyrus had been developed in Egypt. Although we think of papyrus as the predecessor of paper, it is not technically defined as paper because it lacks a paper-making process called fiber liberation. Yet even before the development of papyrus, ancient people were folding sheets of material, whether fabric or large leaves, using certain techniques. If you define origami as the folding of flat materials, its origin is untraceable. Thus, an intriguing mystery remains unsolved. In a general sense, however, origami refers to the traditional practice of folding square sheets of colored paper to make various forms or models.

Today, we see enthusiasts of this traditional handicraft not only in Japan but also all over the world. An active exchange of origami art is taking place worldwide, and the growing population of origami lovers has expanded the interest in diverse new ways of paper folding. The purpose of this book is to show you some models that are representative of the expanding horizons of origami.

To begin with, I would like to introduce you to my origami puzzles. I hope the puzzles provide you and your family with engaging mental exercises and enjoyable handicrafts.

How to Use This Book

This book will introduce you to the art and wonder of origami and help you learn how to fold traditional origami models and make and solve origami puzzles. You'll soon be ready to share your new discoveries, such as cube origami, with your family and friends. The CD-ROM included with this book contains a wealth of information that complements the book, including instructional movies, slideshows of folding techniques, and images of completed origami models. The CD-ROM is compatible with Windows and Macintosh operating systems.

What's on the CD-ROM?

The CD-ROM provides various information that complements the contents of the book.

Folding Symbols Movie

Instructional Flash movies demonstrate each folding symbol to help you understand the techniques that the symbols represent.

Origami Folding Instructions

Instructional Flash movies for folding techniques teach you how to fold all the basic forms from the first to the last steps—all you need to know to make the origami models and puzzles featured in the book.

Fun with Origami

Instructional Flash movies show you how to have fun with origami in motion, including modular origami, origami assemblies, and magic origami—models that change appearance as you manipulate them.

Solutions to Puzzles

Easy-to-understand Flash movies show you the solutions to the puzzles described in the book.

Origami Slide Shows

Slideshows reveal the beauty and wonder that can be created with a 6" X 6" (15 X 15cm) square sheet of paper.

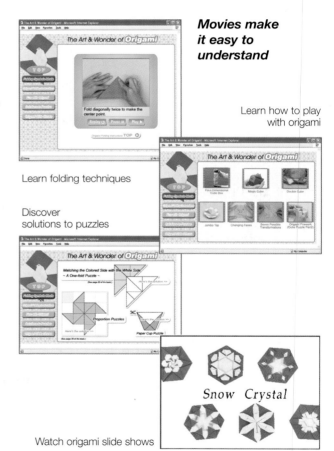

Movies make it easy to understand

Learn how to play with origami

Learn folding techniques

Discover solutions to puzzles

Watch origami slide shows

Snow Crystal

About the Data on the CD-ROM

In addition to the movies and slideshows, the CD-ROM also contains *chiyogami* design data and crease-line data for you to print out and use. Print out the PDF files from the CD-ROM, and use the designs to fold your origami models over and over again.

Original *Chiyogami* Design Collection

The CD-ROM contains 110 styles of original *chiyogami* design sheets that you can use for various origami works, including traditional Japanese designs such as cherry blossoms, fireworks, and Arabesque, as well as general patterns such as cross stripes, polka dots, and animals.

Original *chiyogami* designs

Crease-lined Origami Data Collection

The CD-ROM also contains the data for origami sheets with preprinted crease lines. You can make playful forms easily by just folding along the crease lines according to the instructions. Enjoy these designs with young children, and see if they can guess what form the sheets will make.

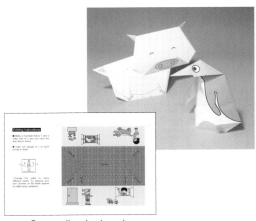

See page 135 for instructions on how to use the Original *Chiyogami* Design Collection and the Crease-lined Origami Data Collection.

Crease-lined origami paper

How to Read the Symbols in This Book

An explanation of the folding techniques and symbols used in this book follows:

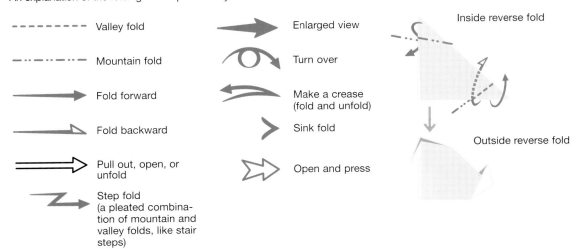

- Valley fold
- Mountain fold
- Fold forward
- Fold backward
- Pull out, open, or unfold
- Step fold (a pleated combination of mountain and valley folds, like stair steps)
- Enlarged view
- Turn over
- Make a crease (fold and unfold)
- Sink fold
- Open and press
- Inside reverse fold
- Outside reverse fold

Other Symbols in This Book

MOVIE This symbol indicates a Flash movie that illustrates the folding technique on the CD-ROM.

SLIDESHOW This symbol indicates a slideshow related to the model on the CD-ROM.

DATA This symbol indicates a PDF file of the crease-lined origami sheet image of the model on the CD-ROM.

How to Use the CD-ROM

Movies and *chiyogami* design sheet data included.

How to Start the CD-ROM

The CD-ROM included with this book is compatible with both Windows and Macintosh operating systems. Use the following instructions to start the CD-ROM, depending on your operating system.

For Windows:

1) Insert the CD-ROM into your computer's CD-ROM drive.
2) Double-click the origami folder in your CD-ROM drive. A window containing the files on the CD-ROM opens.
3) Double-click the file index.html. ———
4) The main page of the file appears.

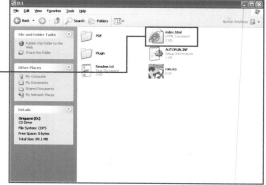

For Macintosh:

1) Insert the CD-ROM into your CD-ROM drive. A window opens automatically.
2) Double-click the file index.html. ———
3) The main page of the file appears.

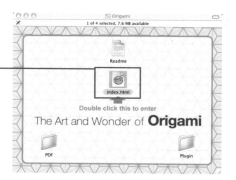

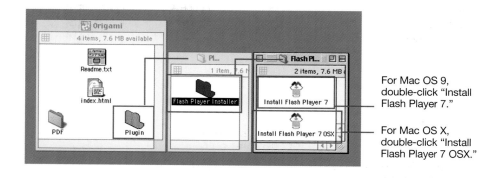

For Mac OS 9, double-click "Install Flash Player 7."

For Mac OS X, double-click "Install Flash Player 7 OSX."

Install Flash Player

To view the CD-ROM you must have Macromedia Flash Player 6 (or higher) installed as a plug-in to your computer's browser software. If the plug-in is not installed, make sure to install it according to the instructions shown. The CD-ROM provides the Flash Player installer in the Flash Player Installer folder in the Plugin folder.

For Netscape, double-click
"flashplayer7_win."

For Internet Explorer, double-click
"flashplayer7_winax."

Enable JavaScript in Your Browser

The CD-ROM contains some JavaScript content. Make sure to enable JavaScript on your browser.

System Requirements

Windows:

OS:	Windows XP/Me/2000/98
CPU:	Pentium 166MHz or faster
Memory:	32 MB or more
Hard disk:	100 MB or more
Monitor:	800 X 600 or better resolution (recommended: 1024 X 768 or higher), more than 65,000 colors
CD-ROM drive:	4x or faster (recommended: 8x or faster)
Browser:	Microsoft Internet Explorer 5.0 or higher Netscape Navigator 4.7 or higher (excluding version 6.0)
Plug-in:	Adobe Acrobat Reader 5.0 or higher Macromedia Flash Player 6 or higher

Macintosh:

OS:	Mac OS 8.6 or higher
CPU:	Power Macintosh
Memory:	32 MB or more
Hard disk:	100 MB or more
Monitor:	800 X 600 or better resolution (recommended: 1024 X 768 or higher), 16-bit color or more
CD-ROM drive:	4x or faster (recommended: 8x or faster)
Browser:	Microsoft Internet Explorer 5.0 or higher Netscape Navigator 4.7 or higher (excluding version 6.0)
Plug-in:	Adobe Acrobat Reader 5.0 or higher Macromedia Flash Player 6 or higher

Important Usage Restrictions and Guidelines

* The data on the CD-ROM may not be accurately displayed or printed, depending on your computer's settings.
* Printing data from the CD-ROM may require the adjustment of your printer's settings. The color tones of the printouts may differ from those shown in this book.
* The author and the publisher of this book accept no responsibility for any damage caused by the data on the CD-ROM.
* Questions regarding the data on the CD-ROM will not be answered by the author or publisher of this book.
* The copyrights and trademark rights of any data on the CD-ROM belong to the author of this book.
* The data on the CD-ROM is for personal use only. Transfer, rental, lease, transmission, and delivery of the data to a third party are prohibited.
* Windows is a registered trademark of Microsoft Corporation in the United States and other countries.

Introduction: Folding Origami

Try Your Hand at Some Easy Models

Here are a few fun and easy-to-make models for beginners.
Try them to exercise all five fingers.

Paper Cup

The Paper Cup is one of the best-known origami of practical use. In Japan, kindergarten children use it for holding their sweets. You may even drink water from it, if you fold it with aluminum foil.

Witches Claws

This model is not traditional. One of the modern Japanese origami pioneers, Kosho Uchiyama, developed a similar model. Here we introduce an easy way to fold it based on his idea.

They will look good on your fingers when folded with regular size origami sheets (6" X 6"; 15 X 15 cm;).

How to Fold
Paper Cup

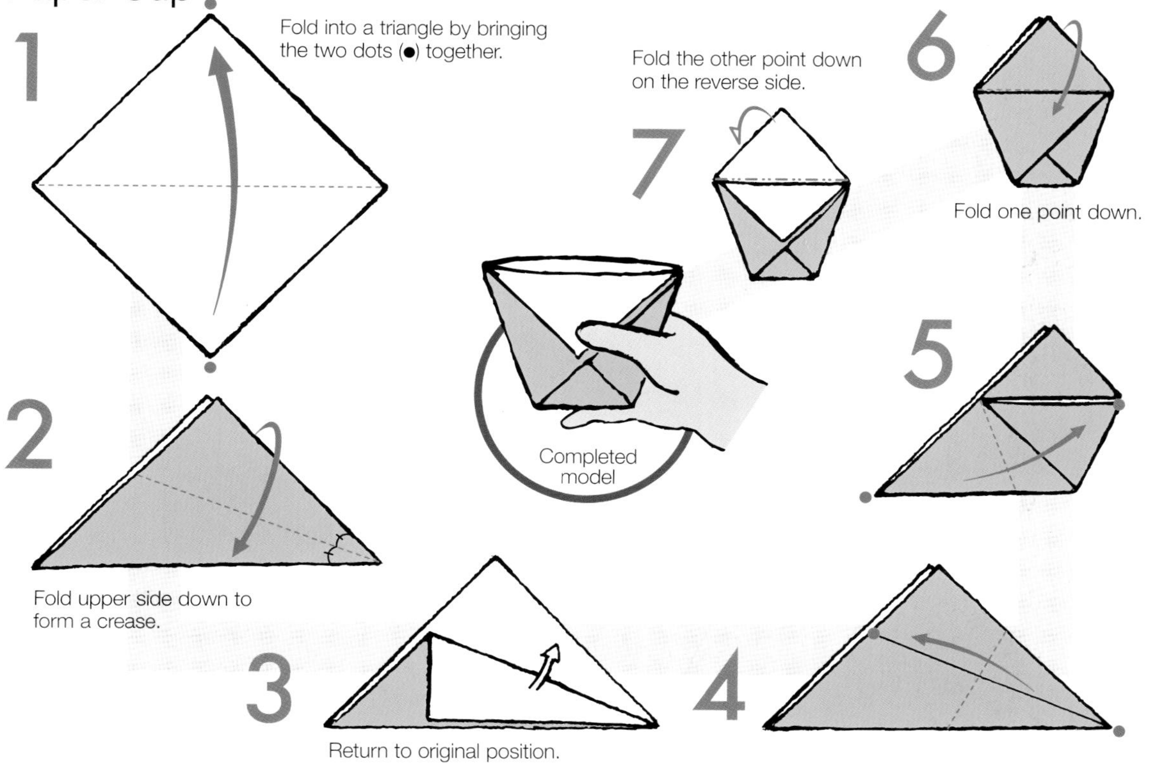

1 Fold into a triangle by bringing the two dots (●) together.

2 Fold upper side down to form a crease.

3 Return to original position.

4

5

6 Fold one point down.

7 Fold the other point down on the reverse side.

Completed model

How to Fold
Witches Claws

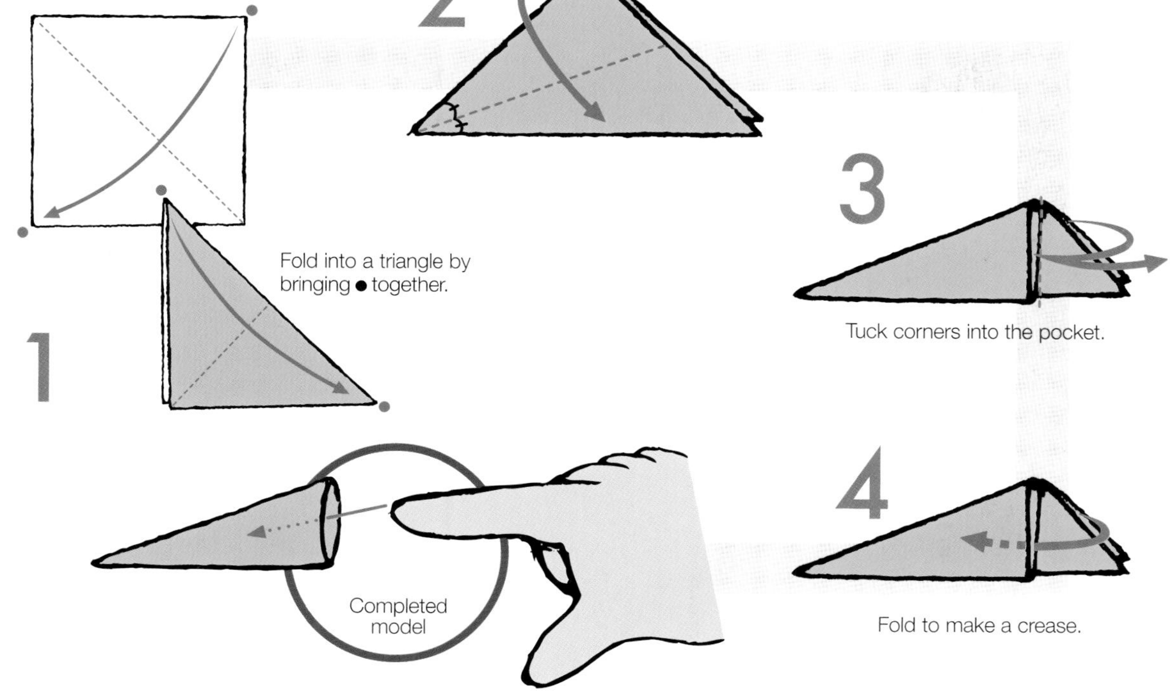

1 Fold into a triangle by bringing ● together.

2

3 Tuck corners into the pocket.

4 Fold to make a crease.

Completed model

Folding with a Variety of Materials

Today, various of materials, including plastic, cloth, clay, and aluminum have become part of the origami world. Even papyrus, the original "paper," has been re-introduced in origami. You can also use wet sheets of leather and fold them with tools such as pliers.

Pinwheel
made of print *chiyogami* paper (a type of Japanese paper decorated with colorful wood block-print patterns)

Container
made of restored papyrus purchased at a large paper shop in San Francisco

Yakko
wearing Japanese kilt made of *chiyogami* paper

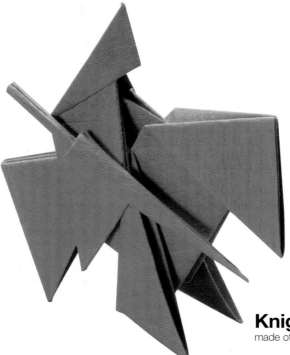

Knight on a Horse
made of western flock paper

Osanpo
made of colored gauze origami (this "colored" mesh was developed by Shoichi Yashimoda)

Pajarita
made of plastic film
"small bird" in Spanish

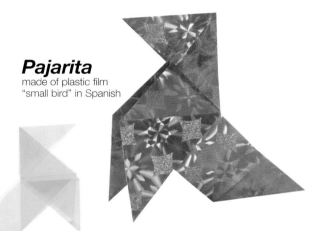

Beniire
made of *washi* (Japanese mulberry paper)

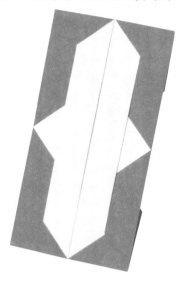

Four Dimensional Cube
made of an origami paper (high-quality).
See page 78 for instructions on making this project.

Folding a *Beniire*

To begin, try folding the *Beniire* from the model featured on page 13.
A *beniire* (meaning gift envelope) is a traditional Japanese purse that ladies
once used for carrying lip rouge. This piece is said to be an ancestral origami
model created by the Maedas, a powerful Japanese family of the sixteenth
century who are now well known thanks to a popular historical drama, *Toshiie
and Matsu* on Japanese TV (NHK, 2002). Today, people like to use the *Beniire*
as a gift-money envelope or a tissue holder. A sheet measuring 9" x 9" (23 x 23
cm) will make an envelope large enough to hold bills.

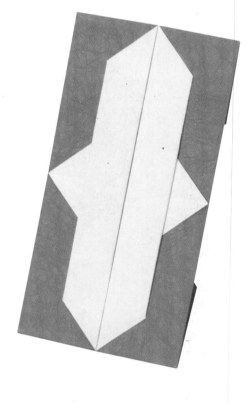

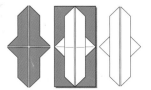

MOVIE

Why Is the *Beniire* So Beautiful?

The beauty of the *Beniire* can be attributed to the symmetry of its colored and white sections, which are
proportionately equal on both the front and back of the envelope.

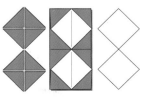

Front   Back

The colored and white sections are symmetrical on both sides.

Beniire

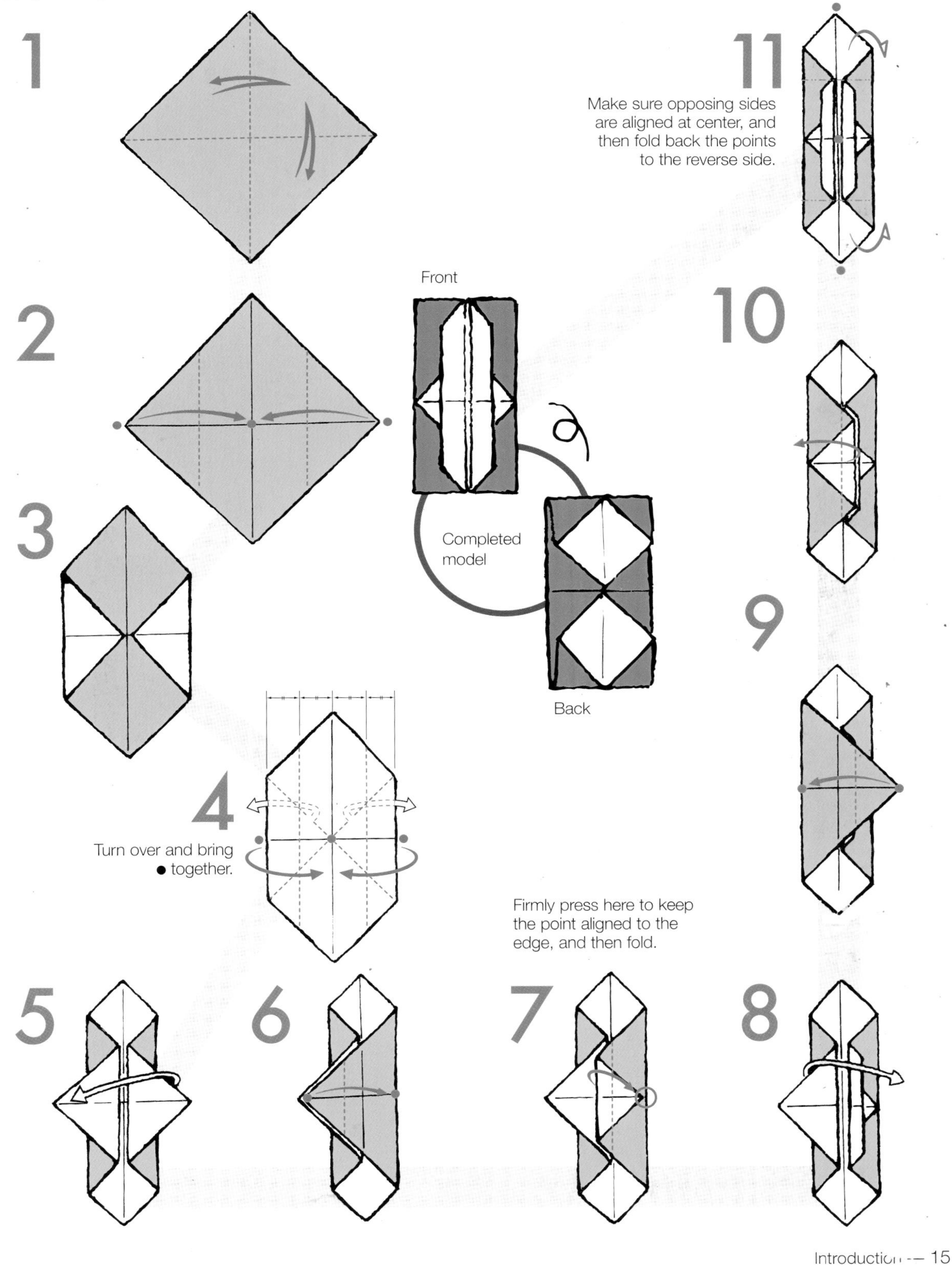

1

2

3

4

Turn over and bring
● together.

5

6

7

Firmly press here to keep
the point aligned to the
edge, and then fold.

8

9

10

11

Make sure opposing sides
are aligned at center, and
then fold back the points
to the reverse side.

Front

Completed
model

Back

Making a Spinning Top Using Several Sheets of Paper

A variation of the previously shown Paper Cup model, this design integrates seven sheets of paper into a single unit. We call this technique "unit origami" or "modular origami." (For details, see chapter 3.)

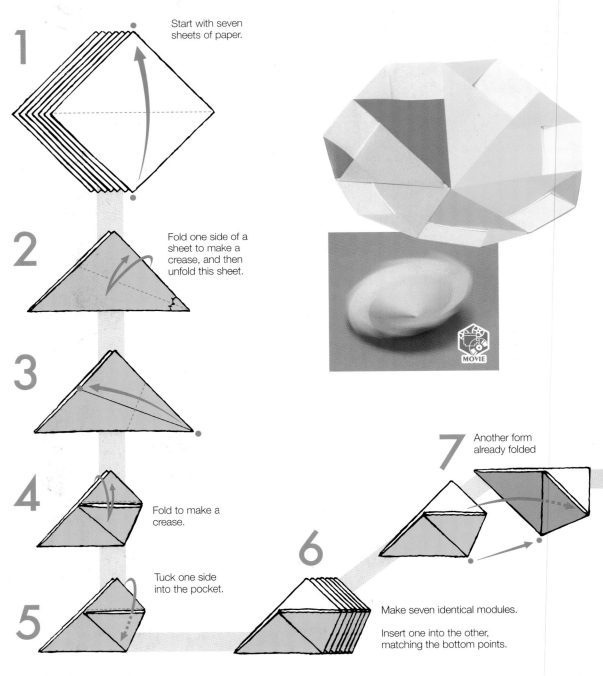

1 Start with seven sheets of paper.

2 Fold one side of a sheet to make a crease, and then unfold this sheet.

3

4 Fold to make a crease.

5 Tuck one side into the pocket.

6

7 Another form already folded

Make seven identical modules.

Insert one into the other, matching the bottom points.

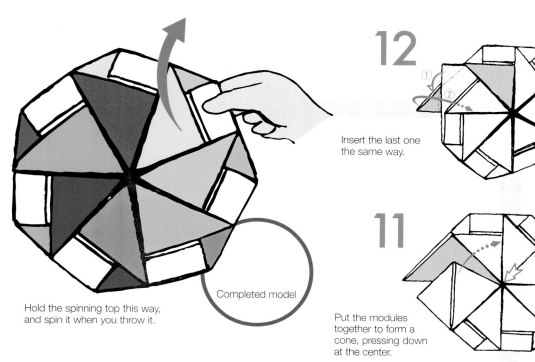

Hold the spinning top this way,
and spin it when you throw it.

Completed model

12

Insert the last one
the same way.

11

Put the modules
together to form a
cone, pressing down
at the center.

9

Third piece

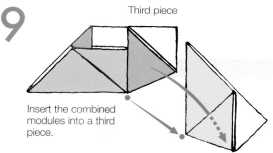

Insert the combined
modules into a third
piece.

10

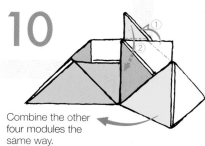

Combine the other
four modules the
same way.

8

Fold this part first.

Then, tuck the point
into the pocket.

How Do You Draw a Regular Heptagon?

Mathematicians know that drawing a regular heptagon, even
with a straightedge and compass, is impossible. But using origami, you can draw the figure without any tools. How amazing is
that?

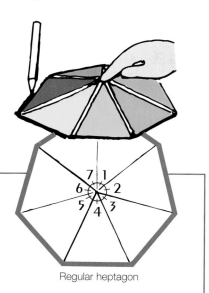

Regular heptagon

Are the Colored and Blank Sections the Same on the Paper Cup, Too?

The geometric beauty of the *Beniire* comes from its equally sized colored and white sections. This is also true for the Paper Cup, although it's not as apparent as with the *Beniire*.

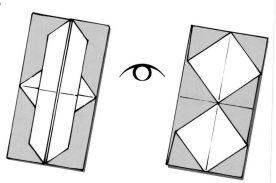

How can you help children understand that the areas of the Paper Cup's colored and white sections are equal in size? You may use scissors to answer this question. (See the CD-ROM for the solution.)

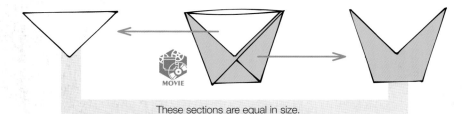

These sections are equal in size.

Another mathematical secret is contained in the Paper Cup. The fourth fold of the Paper Cup model shows that the "S" part of the form is an isosceles triangle. The ratio in size of A to B is 1:2. As you can see, the art of origami is also a means for proving many intriguing geometric and mathematical principles.

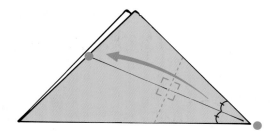

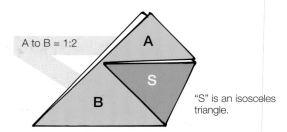

A to B = 1:2

A

S

B

"S" is an isosceles triangle.

Origami Puzzles   Chapter 1

Making the Colored Side Match the White Side with One Fold

Part of the beauty of origami lies in the fact that the colored and white sections of a model are frequently of equal size. This section, offers puzzles that focus that on this aspect of origami.

The colored and white areas of the following six forms—A, B, C, D, E, and F—are not equal. Can you make the colored and white sections equal with one fold? (See the CD-ROM for the solution.)

Easy

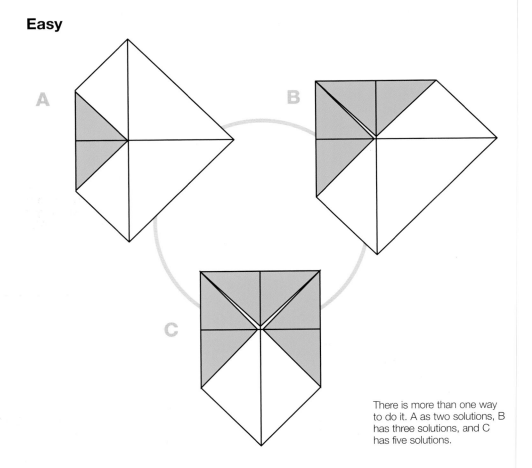

There is more than one way to do it. A as two solutions, B has three solutions, and C has five solutions.

The folding instructions for forms A, B, and C above are on pages 22 and 23.

Challenging

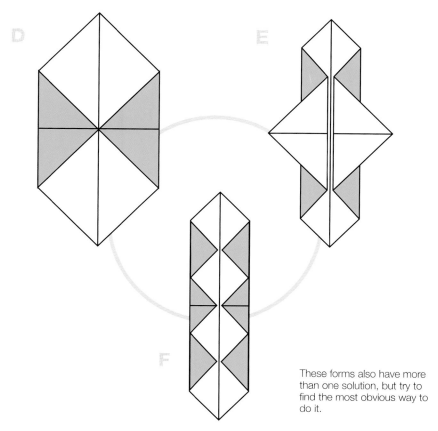

These forms also have more than one solution, but try to find the most obvious way to do it.

How to Solve the One-Fold Puzzle

Use form A as an example of how to follow the rules and work the puzzle, see step 1 and 2 below. Although step 1 seems to have two different answers, each is considered the same solution.

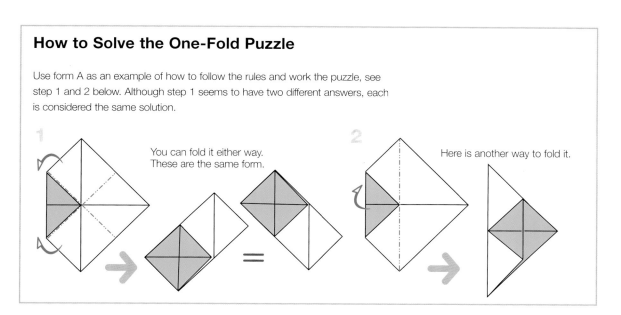

You can fold it either way. These are the same form.

Here is another way to fold it.

How to Make One-Fold Puzzles

Easy

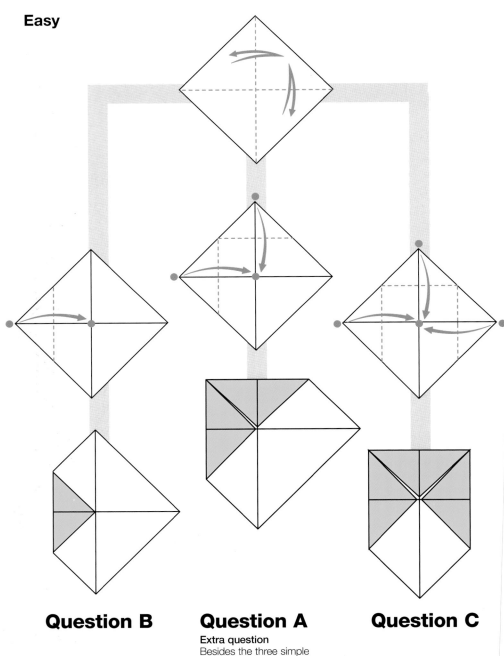

Question B   **Question A**   **Question C**

Extra question
Besides the three simple
solutions, there's another
tricky way to solve B. If
you think you're an origami
whiz, try to find the tricky
solution.

Challenging

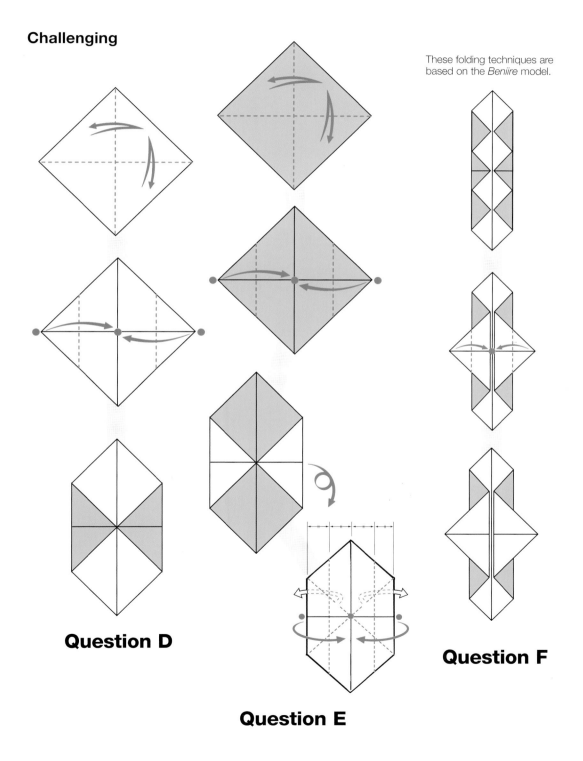

These folding techniques are based on the *Beniire* model.

Question D

Question E

Question F

Puzzles Based on Traditional Origami Models

Among the traditional models there are many variations. Try learning how to fold the variations without referring to instructions. To begin, let's learn how to fold the *Yakko* and the Pinwheel.

Yakko

Pinwheel

Two basic origami models: the *Yakko* and the Pinwheel

Like the Crane, *Yakko-san* (the footman or doorman)—which we call *Yakko*—is synonymous with origami itself. However, little is known about when and where it was first folded, or what it was originally called. The Pinwheel is thought to have originated in Europe.

Yakko

This fold, called the "floor cushion," reduces the size of paper by half; the paper's size is reduced from 1 to ½ to ¼ to ⅛, and so on, at every round of folding.

1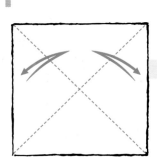

2 ☐ 1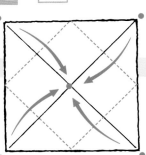

3 ½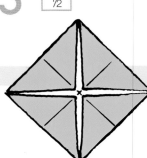

Pinwheel

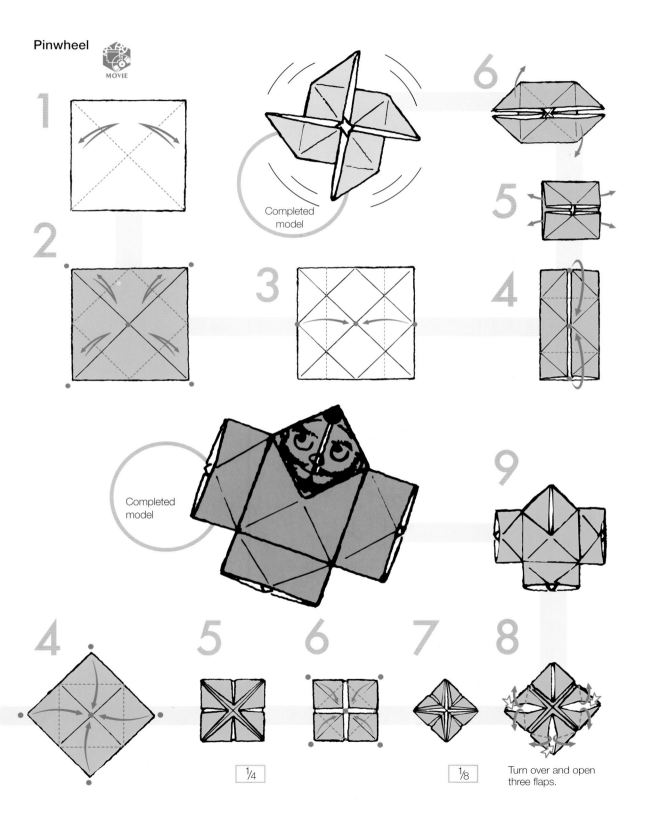

Completed model

Completed model

1

2

3

4

5

6

4

5
1/4

6

7
1/8

8
Turn over and open
three flaps.

9

Variations of the Pinwheel

Now that you have learned how to fold the Pinwheel, try making its variations. How to fold them? That is the puzzle. (See page 122 for the solution.)

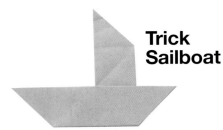

Trick Sailboat

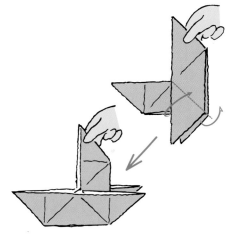

Bring up the points after asking your audience to close their eyes. Then show them that the bow has turned into the sail and the sail into the bow.

Catamaran

Big-Mouthed Fish

Dog (similar to the *Pajarita*)

Boots

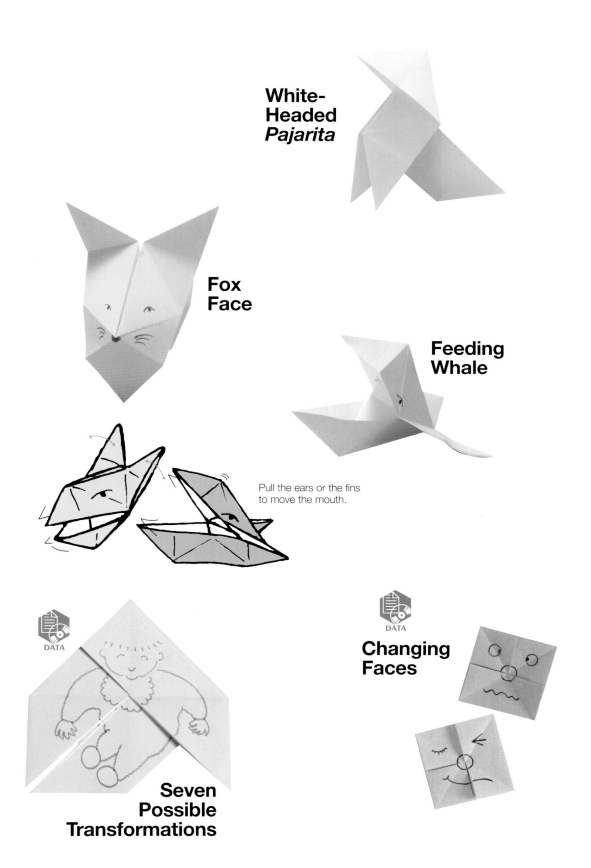

White- Headed *Pajarita*

Fox Face

Feeding Whale

Pull the ears or the fins to move the mouth.

Seven Possible Transformations

DATA

Changing Faces

DATA

Variations of the *Yakko*, Part 1

Some *Yakko* variations follow.
How do you fold them? (See pages 123
and 124 for the solutions.)

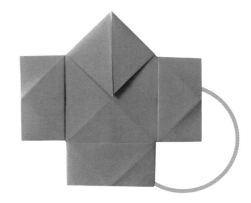

Ghost

**Bon
Festival
Lantern**

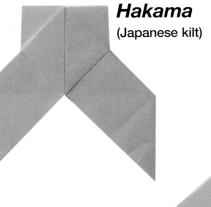

Grand Cross (Germany)
Kakumokkou
Family Emblem
(Japan)

Hakama
(Japanese kilt)

Star

Warship

Sleeve-Waving *Yakko*

Table

Chair B

Chair A

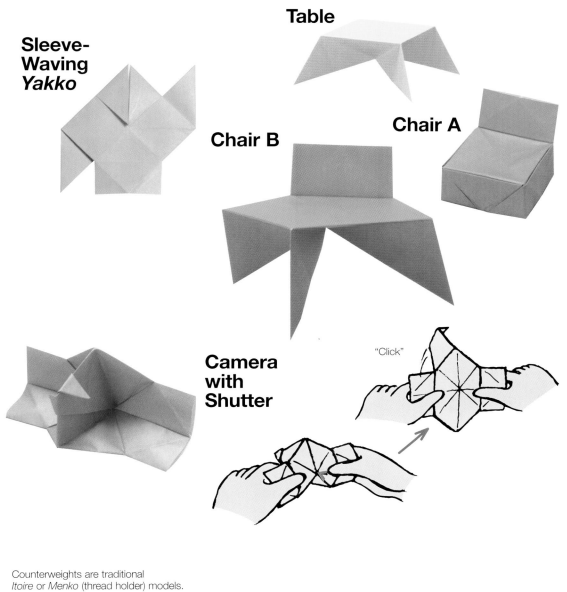

Camera with Shutter

"Click"

Counterweights are traditional *Itoire* or *Menko* (thread holder) models. (See page 33 for instructions.)

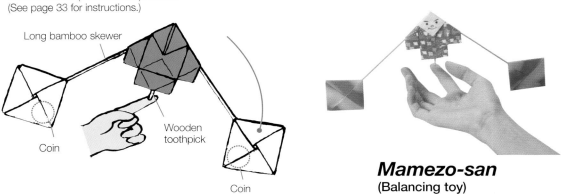

Long bamboo skewer

Coin

Wooden toothpick

Coin

Mamezo-san
(Balancing toy)

Variations of the *Yakko*, Part 2

More *Yakko* variations are shown below.

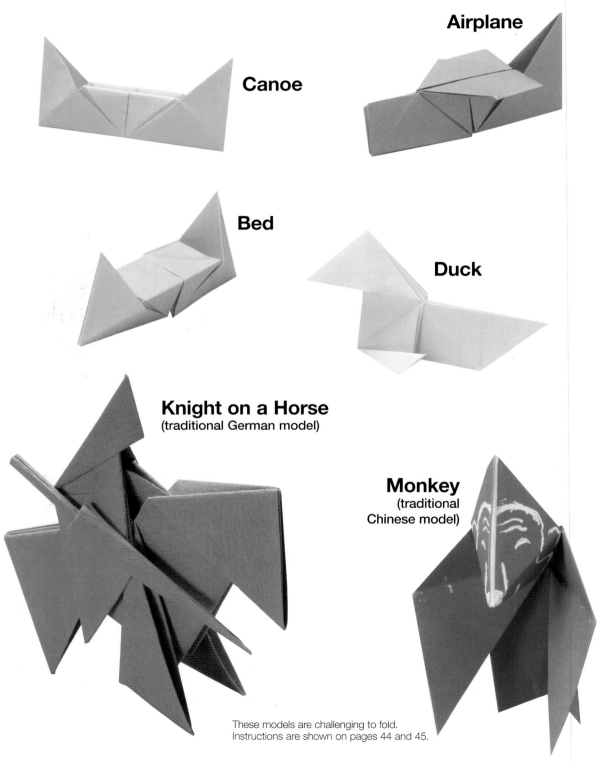

Airplane

Canoe

Bed

Duck

Knight on a Horse
(traditional German model)

Monkey
(traditional
Chinese model)

These models are challenging to fold.
Instructions are shown on pages 44 and 45.

Pajarita ("small bird" in Spanish)

In Spain, the *Pajarita* is the most popular origami model, just as the Crane is in Japan.

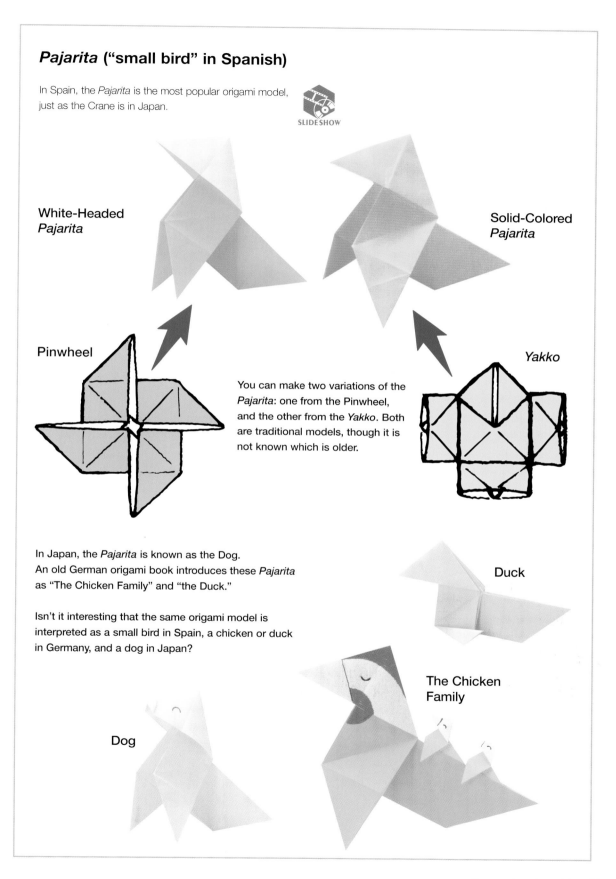

SLIDESHOW

White-Headed *Pajarita*

Solid-Colored *Pajarita*

Pinwheel

You can make two variations of the *Pajarita*: one from the Pinwheel, and the other from the *Yakko*. Both are traditional models, though it is not known which is older.

Yakko

In Japan, the *Pajarita* is known as the Dog. An old German origami book introduces these *Pajarita* as "The Chicken Family" and "the Duck."

Isn't it interesting that the same origami model is interpreted as a small bird in Spain, a chicken or duck in Germany, and a dog in Japan?

Duck

Dog

The Chicken Family

Two Kinds of Pinwheels

In the previous section, you learned about origami puzzles based on the *Yakko* and the Pinwheel. More variations of the Pinwheel are shown here, each with a different divisional proportion for the first fold. Which version do you think is older?

Quarter folds

Third folds

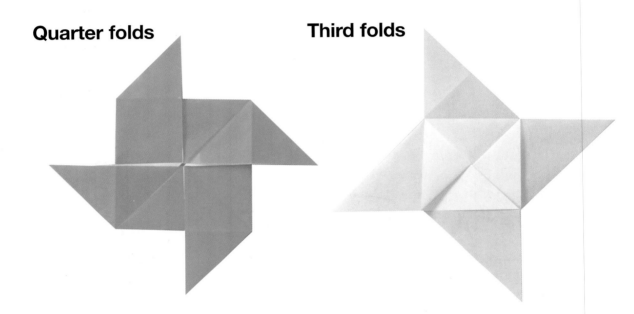

Third-fold Pinwheel (*Itoire,* or thread holder)

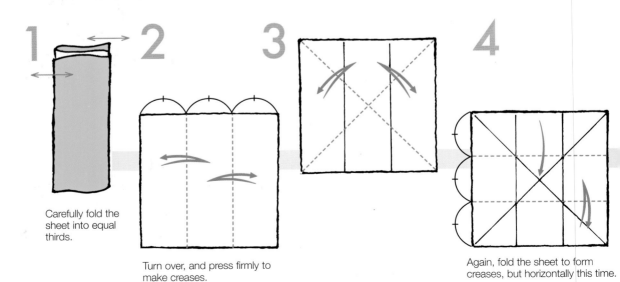

Carefully fold the sheet into equal thirds.

Turn over, and press firmly to make creases.

Again, fold the sheet to form creases, but horizontally this time.

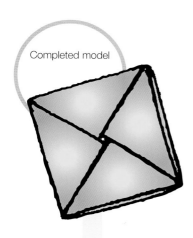

Completed model

From *Itoire* to *Menko*

The third-fold variation of the Pinwheel model was called *Itoire* (thread holder) in the Edo period (1603–1867) and later became *Menko*. The quarter-fold Pinwheel model first appears in some documents from the Meiji period (1868–1912). The quarter-fold variation is believed to have originated in Germany.

Are older origami models more complicated than newer ones?

Historical documents on origami show that the more complicated the models are, the longer they have existed. As far as Pinwheels are concerned, the third-fold version is much more challenging to fold than the quarter-fold version. This "rule" holds true for not only the Pinwheel but also for other models like the *Komosou* (see Chapter 2 for details).

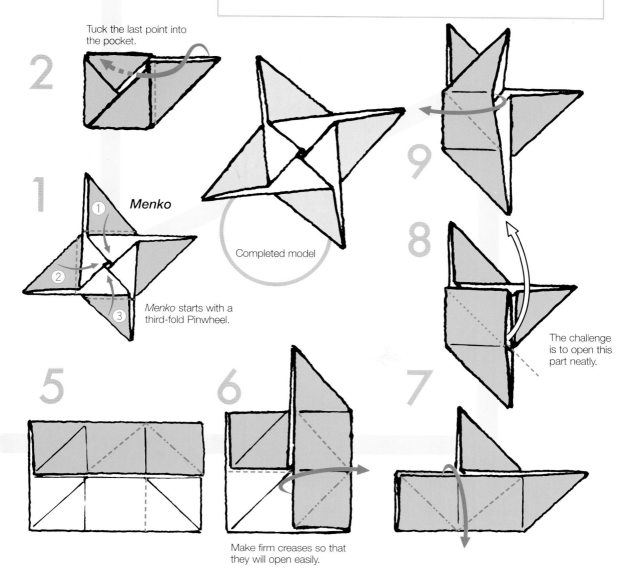

2 — Tuck the last point into the pocket.

1 — *Menko*

Menko starts with a third-fold Pinwheel.

Completed model

9

8 — The challenge is to open this part neatly.

5

6 — Make firm creases so that they will open easily.

7

Determining Proportions

Folded shapes visibly show the proportion of their size to the whole. Therefore, you can use origami to teach children about fractions.

First, let's say the whole square is 1.

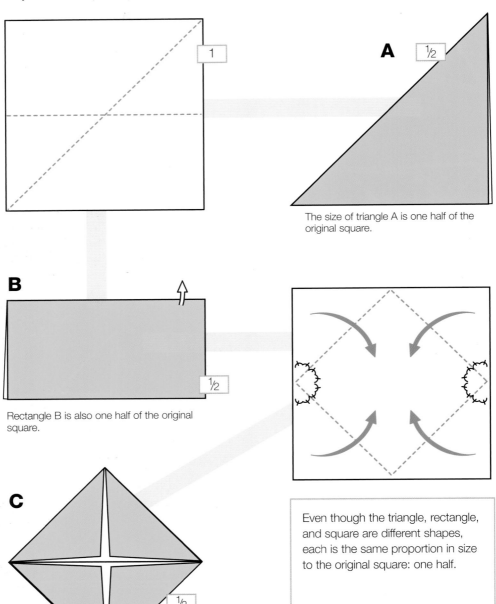

1

A ½

The size of triangle A is one half of the original square.

B

½

Rectangle B is also one half of the original square.

C

½

And so is the size of the Floor Cusion C.

Even though the triangle, rectangle, and square are different shapes, each is the same proportion in size to the original square: one half.

Proportion puzzles

Once you understand the concept introduced on the previous page, try these puzzles. Determine each of the following traditional models' area in proportion to the original square. If the original square's area is 1, what fraction does each model make? The grid on the right may help you find the answers.

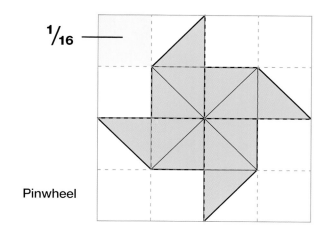

$\frac{1}{16}$

Pinwheel

What fraction of the original square's size is each of these models? (See the CD-ROM for the answers.)

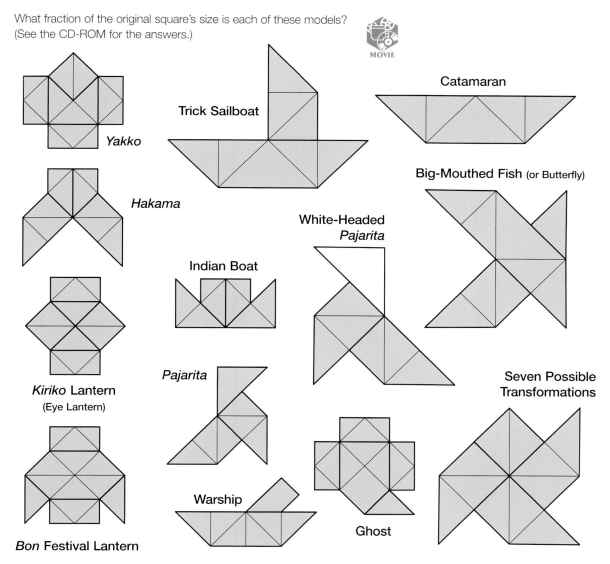

Yakko

Trick Sailboat

Catamaran

Hakama

Big-Mouthed Fish (or Butterfly)

White-Headed
Pajarita

Indian Boat

Kiriko Lantern
(Eye Lantern)

Pajarita

Seven Possible
Transformations

Warship

Ghost

Bon Festival Lantern

Partial Inversion Puzzle

Once you feel comfortable making the *Yakko* model, try making a white part appear on a colored part using the partial inversion technique. It's like a puzzle. An example of a partial inversion puzzle follows.

Completed model

White-Faced *Yakko*

1

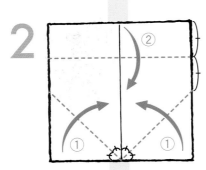

2

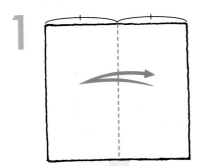

3

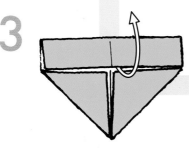

Unfold the top portion of the sheet.

4

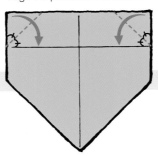

Align the points on the crease.

5

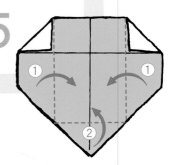

6

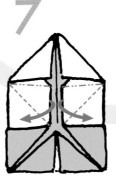

7

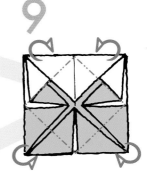

8

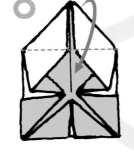

9

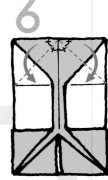

10

How do you fold these models? (See pages 125–134 for the solutions.)
For the original folding techniques without inversion, see the next page.

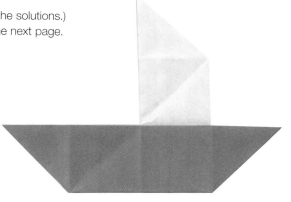

Hakama with a White Waistband

Boat with a White Sail

This excellent puzzle was found on the Origami Tanteidan website (http://origami.gr.jp/) on March 18, 2001. It is a model folded by "h.k." I send him or her big round of applause.

Sleeve-Waving *Yakko* with a White Face

Yakko with a White Waist

Bon Festival Lantern with a White Body

These two models are challenging.
Try them before checking the instructions in the back of the book.

Kiriko Lantern (Eye Lantern) with a White Body

Original folds without inversion

You must know how to fold the original models before trying the partial inversion puzzles on the previous page. The instructions for the originals follow. (See page 24 for *Yakko*.) Master these models first, and then go ahead and explore the variations.

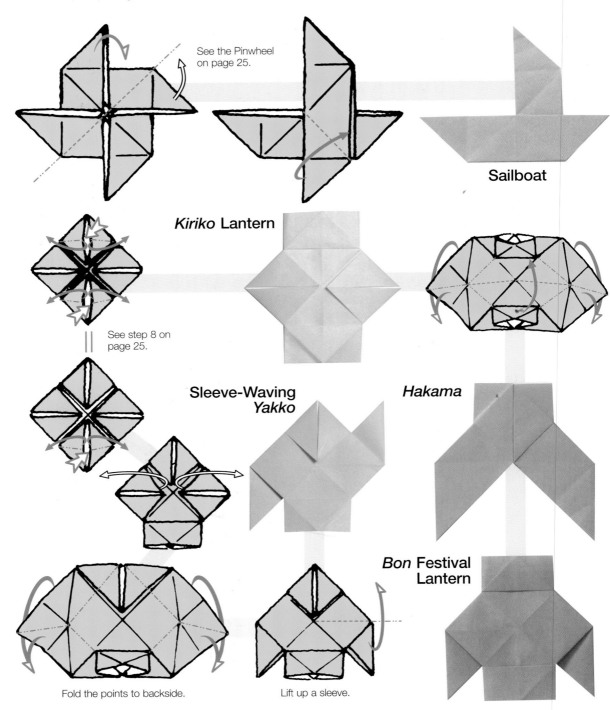

See the Pinwheel on page 25.

Sailboat

Kiriko Lantern

See step 8 on page 25.

Sleeve-Waving
Yakko

Hakama

Bon Festival
Lantern

Fold the points to backside.

Lift up a sleeve.

Small changes make big challenges.

All the partial inversion puzzles shown on the previous pages are developed from the *Yakko* base. At first I thought they would not differ greatly in difficulty, but after trying the puzzles, I soon realized I was wrong. Even small differences in appearance can make the folds tremendously difficult. However, that's what makes the puzzles exciting. The eye part of the Eye Lantern was so difficult to fold that I almost gave up.

For each model, the inversion is made on the face in the same manner. The only difference is the sleeve; one raises it, whereas the other lets it hang down. See how much this small difference affects the difficulty of folding?

Easy   **Difficult**

The stamp fits in here.

Stamp Box

An interesting book—recommended by Masatsugu Tsutsumi, an origami lover from Kyushu, Japan—is *Paper Toy Making** by Margaret W. Campbell. In it Campbell introduces many of her origami models, including the Stamp Box (left), which is the Gift Box I will show you in Chapter 2, and her Horse and Rider (below). See how lovely the model is, and note how the rider's face is folded using inversion.

*Dover Publications Inc. Reprinted in 1975. (First edition, 1937)

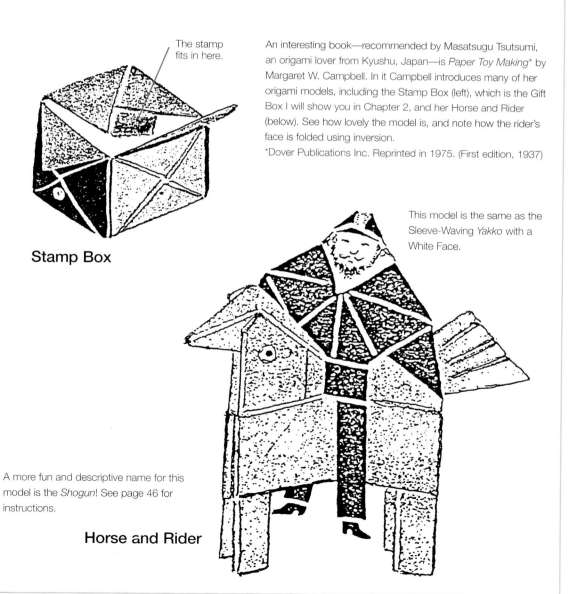

This model is the same as the Sleeve-Waving *Yakko* with a White Face.

A more fun and descriptive name for this model is the *Shogun*! See page 46 for instructions.

Horse and Rider

Octagon Pendant

This book's discussion of origami puzzles has come to a close, but an essential origami puzzle never ends. We may say that the art of origami is itself a profound puzzle, as one small change to an original model can lead to a plethora of variations. The Octagon Pendant is another such variation developed from a basic form. It is popular among kindergarteners in Japan and often accompanies their activities. The model was created by the famous German educator, Friedrich Wilhelm August Froebel (1782–1852), about 150 years ago. It is one of the basic forms that he invented for children (more details on page 42). Unlike other basic forms, this one has survived many years in Japan. Its popularity and longevity is partly because its center looks like a chrysanthemum, a flower the Japanese have historically loved. Another reason is perhaps because of its geometric beauty, featuring one octagon inside another. Japan is said to have many geometry fans. The Octagon Pendant is a masterpiece because it achieves a remarkable balance of practicality and geometric design.

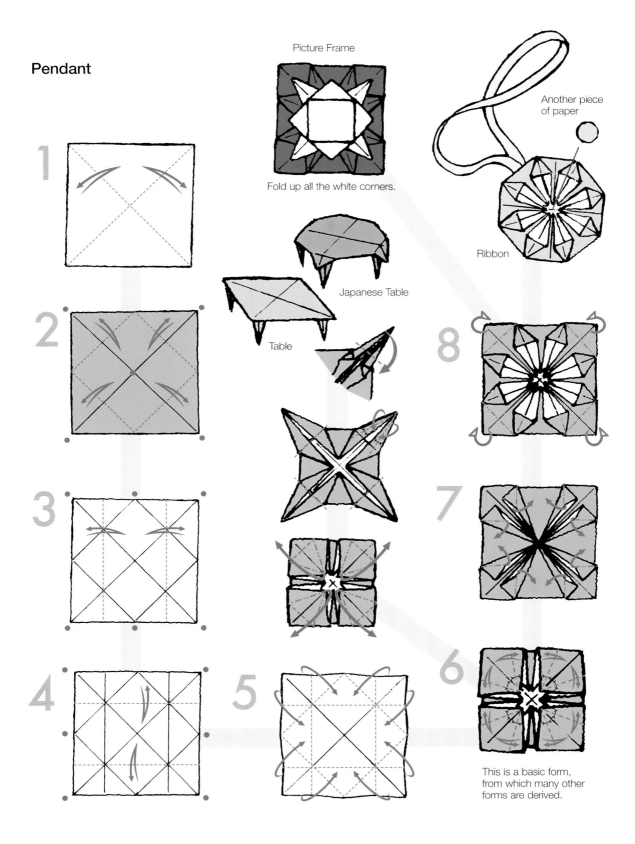

Pendant

1

Picture Frame

Fold up all the white corners.

Another piece of paper

Ribbon

2

Japanese Table

Table

3

8

4

5

7

6

This is a basic form, from which many other forms are derived.

Beautiful Pattern Folds (Basic Forms)

At the end of Chapter 1, you learned about origami models called basic forms. As was previously mentioned, basic forms were developed for young children by the famous German educator Friedrich Froebel (who also originated the kindergarten system). The form shown below is similar to the Octagon Pendant shown on the previous page. However, with just a small change in the folding pattern, the form amazingly reveals beautiful new patterns. Froebel, noting how enjoyable and interesting this folding technique is, encouraged children to discover new designs and learn to make their own. Try folding the forms shown below, and then go ahead and create your own designs. Maybe you'll create a model that has never been seen before.

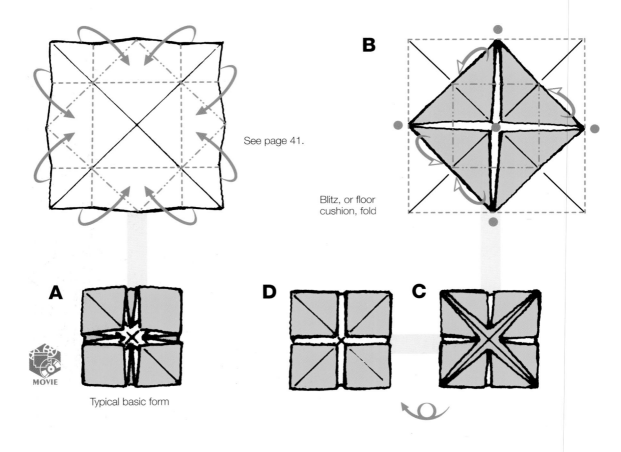

B

See page 41.

Blitz, or floor cushion, fold

A

MOVIE

Typical basic form

D

C

A is one of the common basic forms, but you can also develop many versions from B, C, and D. You can also create beautiful patterns using a sheet of paper cut into equilateral triangles or regular hexagons (see Chapter 2 for details).

Froebel's Basic Forms

These basic forms were developed from model A on the previous page.

Knight on a Horse
(Traditional German Model)

Alice Grey from the United States taught me how to fold this model. Some time later, while visiting a toy museum in Nuremberg, Germany, I saw similar enamel-coated models, exhibited as "Marching Soldiers," that were made some 100 years ago.

Knight
(use a larger sheet of paper for the Knight model)

1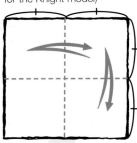

The larger sheet is twice the size of the smaller.

Horse

1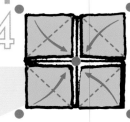

Start with a sheet of paper that is the same size as the one in step 3.

2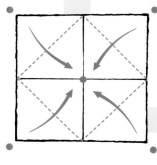

3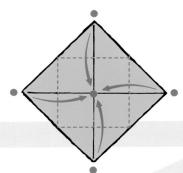

4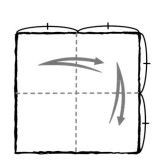

Fold the same way as for the *Yakko* up to this step.

5

6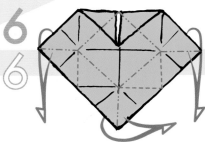

Fold the same way as for the larger sheet up to this step.

7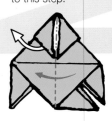

Monkey
(Traditional Chinese Model)

This model is based on a design that appears in *The Art of Chinese Paper Folding* (reprinted edition) and was created by Maying Soong. The first edition of the book was published in 1948 by Harcourt, Brace and Company.

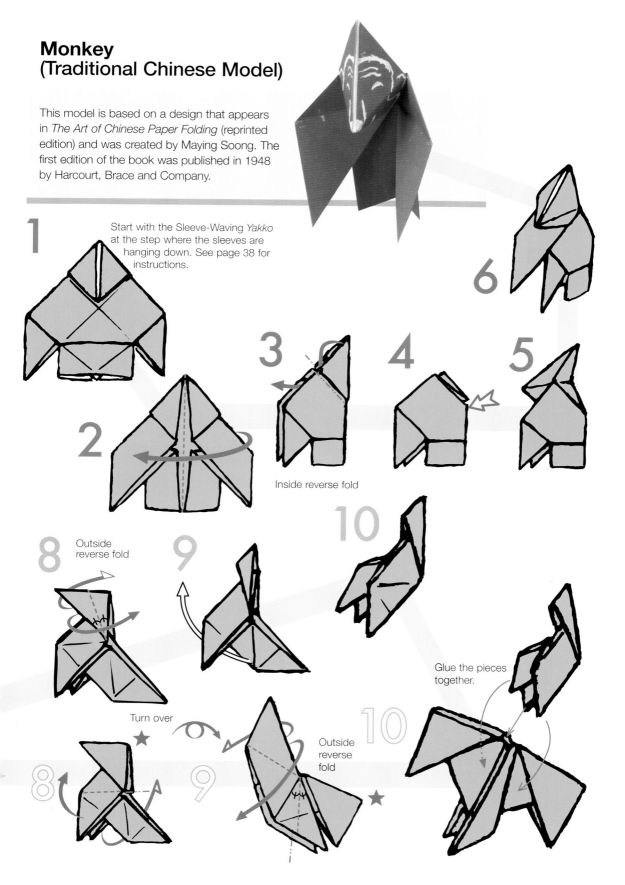

1 Start with the Sleeve-Waving *Yakko* at the step where the sleeves are hanging down. See page 38 for instructions.

2

3

4 Inside reverse fold

5

6

8 Outside reverse fold

9

10

8

9 Turn over

9 Outside reverse fold

10 Glue the pieces together.

Horse and Rider

The Sleeve-Waving *Yakko* with an inverted white head makes a nice rider for the Horse and Rider. You have already learned this model in the puzzle section; Refer to the solution pages in the back of the book for instructions.

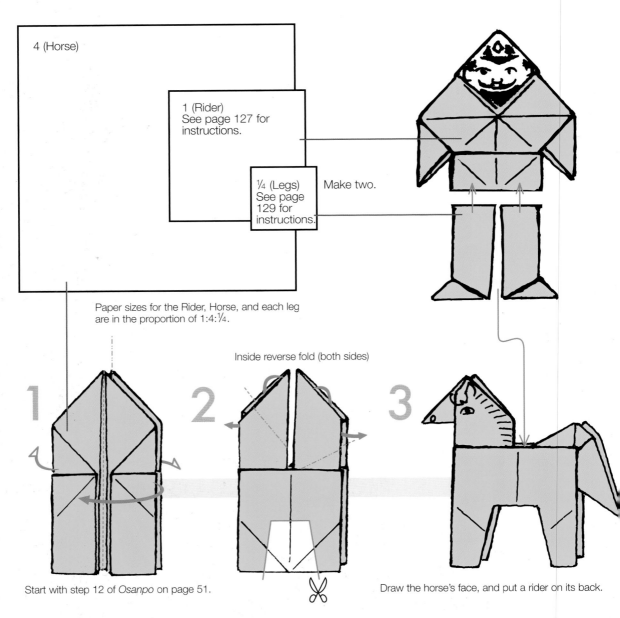

4 (Horse)

1 (Rider)
See page 127 for instructions.

¼ (Legs)
See page 129 for instructions.

Make two.

Paper sizes for the Rider, Horse, and each leg are in the proportion of 1:4:¼.

1

2 Inside reverse fold (both sides)

3

Start with step 12 of *Osanpo* on page 51.

Draw the horse's face, and put a rider on its back.

New Discoveries:
Origami Masterpieces of the Edo Period
Chapter 2

Origami from 270-Year-Old Documents
*Ranma Zushiki**

Origami in the Edo Period (1603–1867)

In April 1993, the Nippon Origami Association (NOA) published a special edition of its monthly journal, *Origami*, to commemorate the NOA's 20th anniversary. The journal was published in the form of a valuable and elegant book by Satoshi Takagi called *Origami from the Classics*, which contained a great deal of information about origami gathered from ancient documents. The book's most fascinating contribution, however, is a print from *Ranma-Zushiki* (right). Edited by Hayato Ohoka in 1734, *Ranma-Zushiki* is a three-volume anthology of Edo-period designs for Japanese hand-carved wooden *ranma* (decorative panels). Historian Yasuo Koyanagi discovered the print called *Origata*, or fold models, in this anthology, and Takagi helped spread public awareness of it with his book.

The Mystery of Six Origami Models

Depicted in the *Ranma Zushiki* print are the following six origami models:

1. Crane
2. *Komosou* (Zen monk wearing deep straw hat)
3. Cargo Boat
4. Cube (the *Tamatebako*)
5. *Ashitsuki-Sanpo* (Offering Case with legs)
6. *Tsuno Kobako* (Perfume Box with Petals or Star Box)

Accompanying the illustration were the following descriptions by Ohoka (quoted according to Mr. Takagi's interpretation):
"There are a variety of designs for fold models. Popular examples include (1) the Crane, (2) *Komosou*, (3) the Cargo Boat, (4) the *Tamatebako*, and (5) a sort of folded pouch for perfume."

At first, the relationship between Ohoka's descriptions and the models shown in the illustration were unclear because he did not include the *Osanpo* (a ceremonial offering case without legs). However, Satoshi Takagi and Masao Okamura, a leading origami historian, helped resolve this mystery. A more complete story about these ancient models is told on the following pages.

* A three-volume anthology of traditional Japanese hand-carved wooden panels, or *ranma* designs, published in 1734.

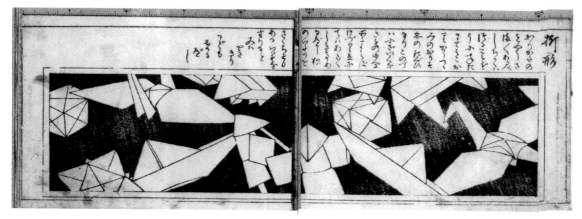

Reprinted courtesy of Satoshi Takagi.

Please note that some parts of the models that are missing in the original print have been restored by the author (the dotted lines).

1. Crane

This model is so popular that it requires no explanation.

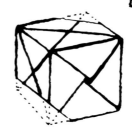

2. *Komosou*

This *Komosou*, meaning one of a loosely knit sect of wandering Zen monks of the late sixteenth century who played the *shakuhachi*, a kind of flute, for donations and wore a face-obscuring straw hat differs from a traditional form known as *Komusou* today. (See page 52 for more detail.)

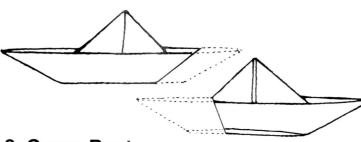

3. Cargo Boat

This model has long been popular in Europe. Today, people enjoy folding this model with newspaper to make paper hats.

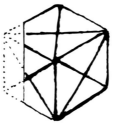

4. Cube *(Tamatebako)*

This lost masterpiece has finally been rediscovered.

See the following page for (5) the *Ashitsuki-Sanpo* and (6) the *Tsuno Kobako*.

Origami Study: *Osanpo*

When you look closely at the illustration from *Ranma-Zushiki* on the previous page, you may notice that the *Osanpo* (a ceremonial offering case) is drawn from three different angles, whereas the other models are drawn from only two angles. The drawing in the bottom-left corner of the print, which is of *Osanpo*, looks like a sixth model. However, this sixth model is not mentioned in Ohoka's description.

When I first saw the drawing, I mistook this sixth model for a cube with triangular pyramids on each plane and tried to fold it myself. (The result is the invention on page 56.) Unaware of my misunderstanding, I presented my invention publicly as a restoration of the model in *Ranma-Zushiki*. Soon after, both Takagi and Okamura contacted me to point out my mistake, saying that what I regarded as a sixth model is in fact the *Tsuno Kobako* viewed from above. Well, that was true.

According to this new interpretation, the *Tsuno Kobako* is correctly identified in Ohoka's description as a "folded pouch for perfume." But I still wonder why the *Osanpo* is the only model drawn from three different angles.

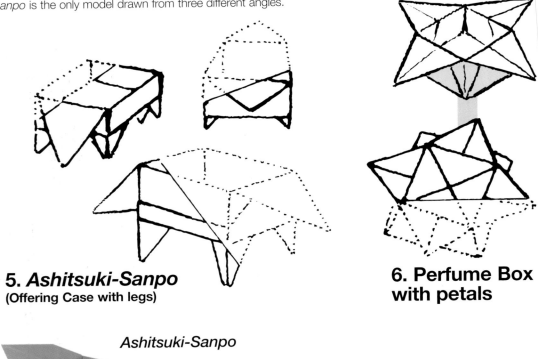

5. *Ashitsuki-Sanpo*
(Offering Case with legs)

6. Perfume Box with petals

Ashitsuki-Sanpo

Osanpo

Osanpo and *Ashitsuki-Sanpo*

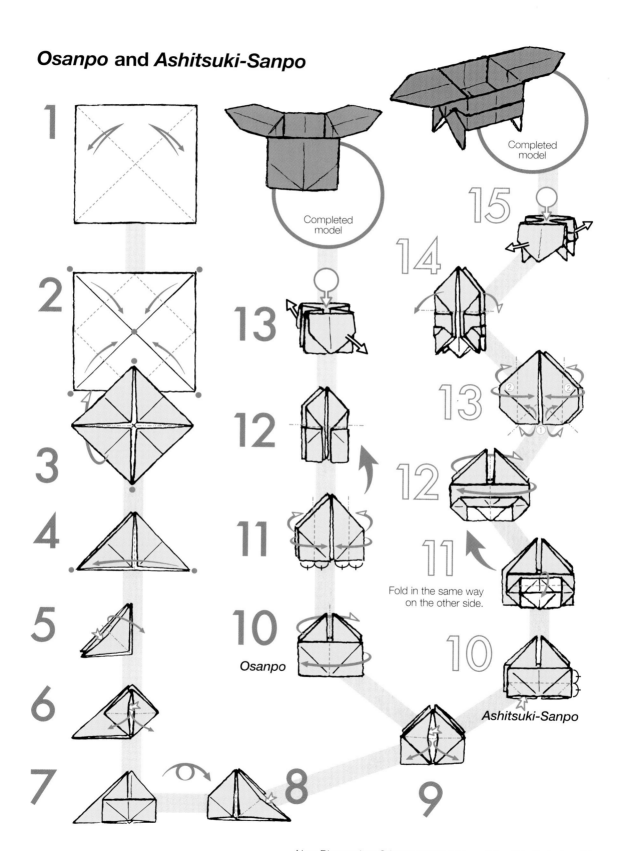

1

2

3

4

5

6

7

8

9

10
Osanpo

11

12

13

Completed
model

15

14

13

12

11
Fold in the same way
on the other side.

10
Ashitsuki-Sanpo

Completed
model

From Historic Documents:
What Is *Komosou*?

As noted on page 24, the origin of the *Yakko* is a mystery. Although it is now synonymous with origami itself in Japan, we know little about when and where it was first folded. Satoshi Takagi is perhaps the first to raise such questions about the *Yakko*. He first points out that the *Komusou* model should be taken for the *Komosou* we know today.

Komusou and *Komosou*, which are thought to be traditional variations of the *Yakko*, often appear in fine art of the Edo period. However, these models were not called *Yakko* in the Edo period. *Yakko* came to be known during the Meiji period, only after Froebel's origami books (see page 40 for more detail) were introduced to Japan.

Ranma-Zushiki reveals that what is today know as *Komusou* was called *Komosou* in those days. When you look at the drawings of *Komusou/Komosou* below (*Ranma* A), you can see that the model looks the same as the *Yakko*. However, *Ranma* B and C, which are taken from older literature, require more complicated folding techniques than the *Yakko*.

Some people consider these drawings to be exaggerated or imaginatively created by an artist of the times. However, as was suggested in Chapter 1 (page 33), traditional folding techniques were complicated at first and then became more simple over time. Thus, it is no wonder that the original *Yakko* was folded using more complicated techniques.

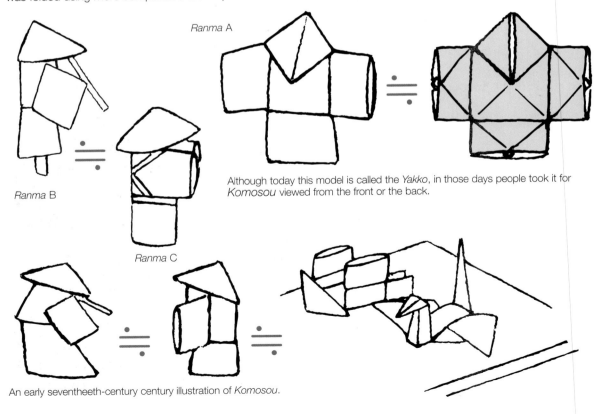

Ranma A

Ranma B

Ranma C

Although today this model is called the *Yakko*, in those days people took it for *Komosou* viewed from the front or the back.

An early seventheeth-century century illustration of *Komosou*.

Komosou and Komusou

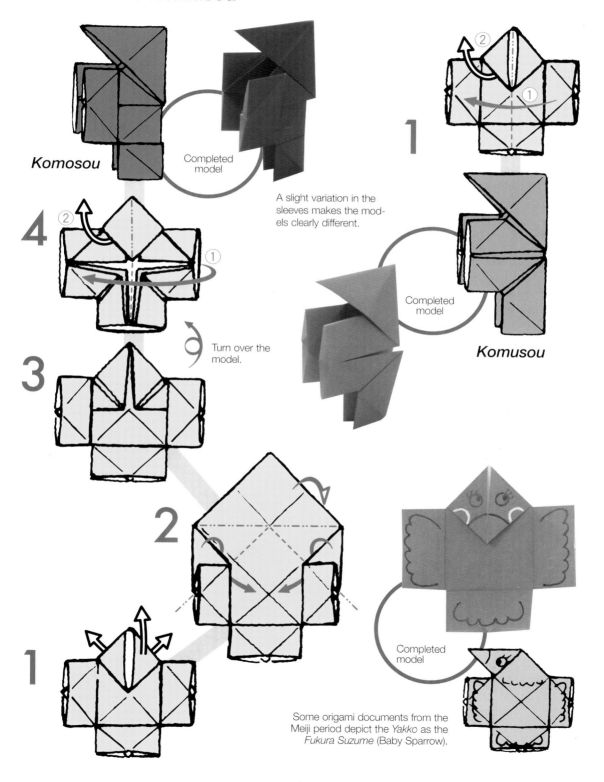

Komosou

Completed model

A slight variation in the sleeves makes the models clearly different.

Komusou

Completed model

1

4

2

3

Turn over the model.

2

1

Completed model

Some origami documents from the Meiji period depict the *Yakko* as the *Fukura Suzume* (Baby Sparrow).

From Historic Documents:
Is This the Original *Komosou*?

Some people say that traditional models from the old age of origami are simple and easy to fold whereas modern models are highly sophisticated and advanced. As you see on the previous page, however, this view is not true at all.

When you look at origami documents from the Edo period, you encounter challenging pieces that require complicated folding techniques on almost every page. With this in mind, I folded a variation of *Ranma-Zushiki's Komosou*, which looks similar to a model in *Contemporary Designs: Models in Detail,** a book published thirty years before *Ranma-Zushiki*. The model is called *Orisue Komosou*, or Standing Monk Bending Down, Model No.106. While folding this piece, I referred to the drawing shown below, believing that it is not an artist's exaggeration but an accurate depiction. Whatever the truth may be, I am confident that this model, which I named *Takuhatsusou*, or the Friar, is a nice work of origami.

*A book published in 1705, according to *Origami from the Classics* (Satoshi Takagi, Nippon Origami Association).

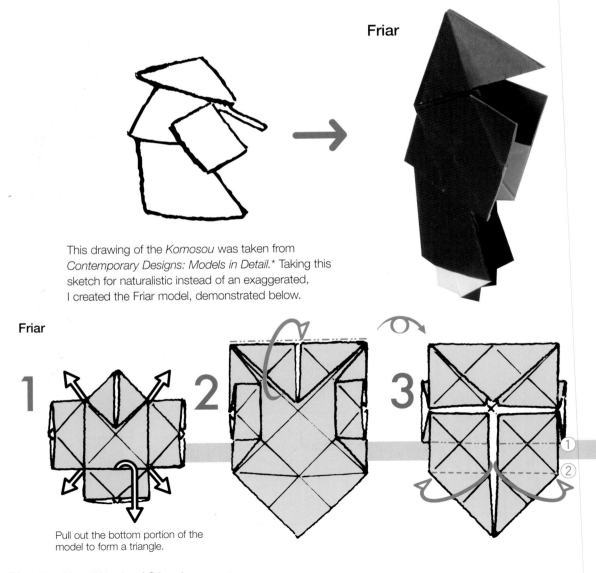

Friar

This drawing of the *Komosou* was taken from *Contemporary Designs: Models in Detail.** Taking this sketch for naturalistic instead of an exaggerated, I created the Friar model, demonstrated below.

Friar

1

2

3

Pull out the bottom portion of the model to form a triangle.

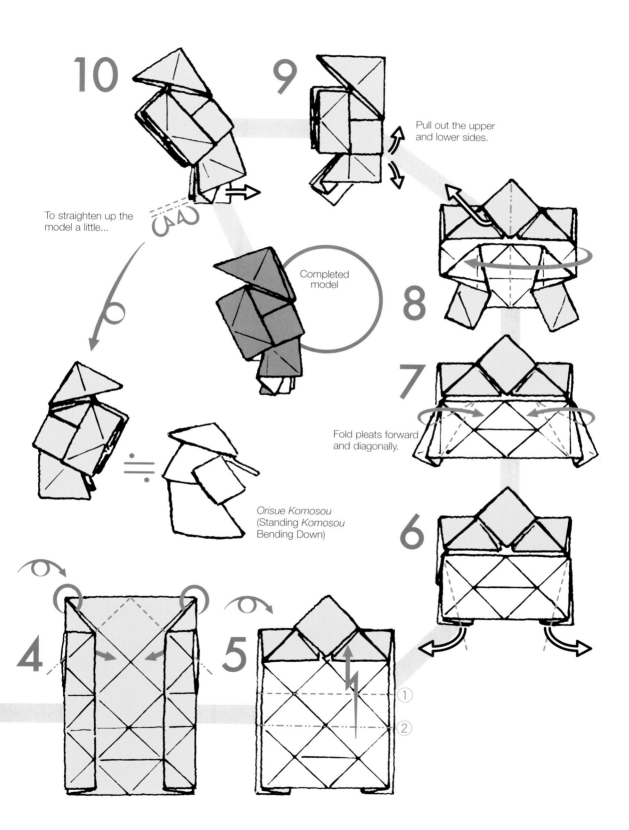

10

9

Pull out the upper and lower sides.

To straighten up the model a little...

Completed model

8

7

Fold pleats forward and diagonally.

Orisue Komosou (Standing *Komosou* Bending Down)

6

4

5

①

②

From Historic Documents: Developing Better Technique

When I first saw the *Tsuno Kobako*, I mistook it for a cube with triangular pyramids on each face and tried to fold the form. The result is the solid figure shown on the right. It was a real puzzle for me to fold this cube because the drawing in *Ranma-Zushiki* shows only the upper half of the model. The model shown on the right was born from my misunderstanding, but I consider it a successful misunderstanding because I have invented this interesting and decorative cube.

Decorative Cube

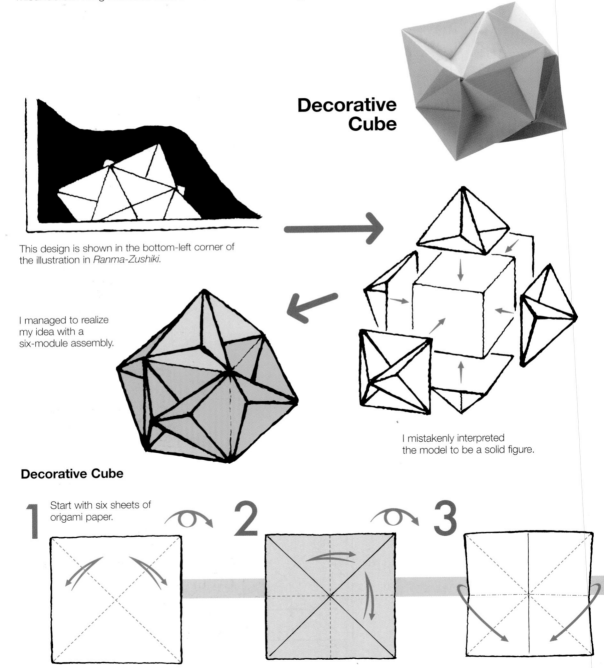

This design is shown in the bottom-left corner of the illustration in *Ranma-Zushiki*.

I managed to realize my idea with a six-module assembly.

I mistakenly interpreted the model to be a solid figure.

Decorative Cube

1 Start with six sheets of origami paper.

2

3

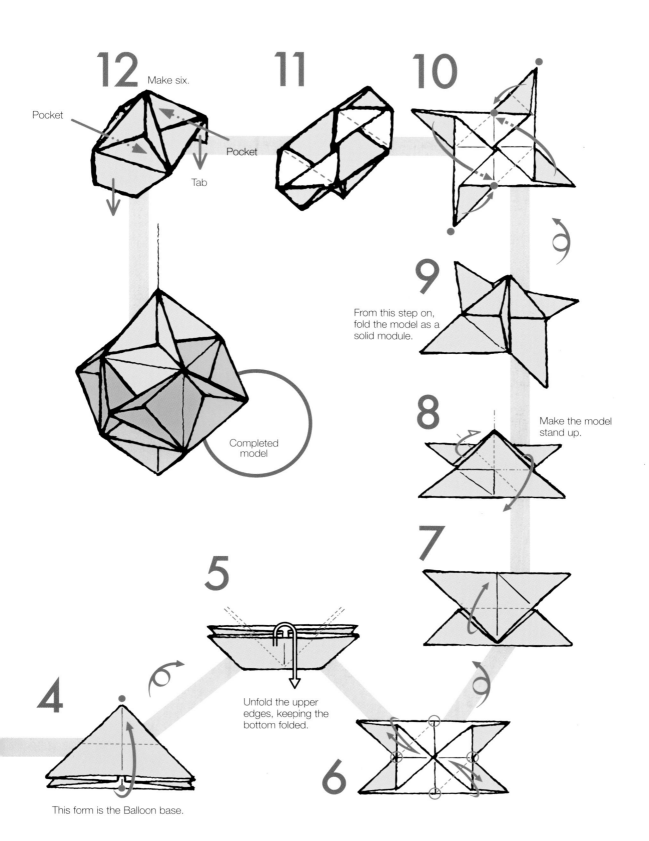

12 Make six.

Pocket

Pocket

Tab

Completed model

11

10

9 From this step on, fold the model as a solid module.

8 Make the model stand up.

7

5 Unfold the upper edges, keeping the bottom folded.

4 This form is the Balloon base.

6

From Historic Documents:
Grand Masterpiece—*Tamatebako*

It is the *Tamatebako*, or Gift Box—which is actually a Cube—that makes *Ranma-Zushiki* most interesting. At first glance, each face of the cube appeared like the traditional *Menko*. So when I tried to restore the *Tamatebako*, I understood it to be a modular origami using *Menko* modules. Though my idea was valid in restoring the model's appearance, I missed the original piece's functional structure. In fact, the *Tamatebako* is not a merely a cube, but a cube that can be opened from any face. Some documents of the Meiji period and origami master Isao Honda's books in the early Showa period (1926–1988) recorded this piece as the *Tamatebako*. A pioneer of modern origami, Honda also discovered a variation of the *Tamatebako*, a cube with a regular hexahedral outline with all eight points faceted. A *Nishikie* wood print that captures the hexahedral version indicates that it was actually used as a container.

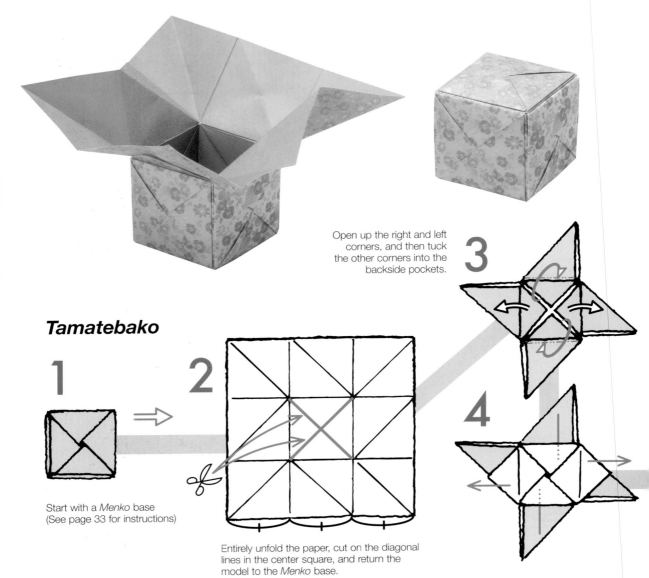

Open up the right and left corners, and then tuck the other corners into the backside pockets.

3

Tamatebako

1

Start with a *Menko* base
(See page 33 for instructions)

2

Entirely unfold the paper, cut on the diagonal lines in the center square, and return the model to the *Menko* base.

4

Tamatebako with Hexahedral Sides

This example shows a later variation of *Tamatebako* with improvements to the folding technique.

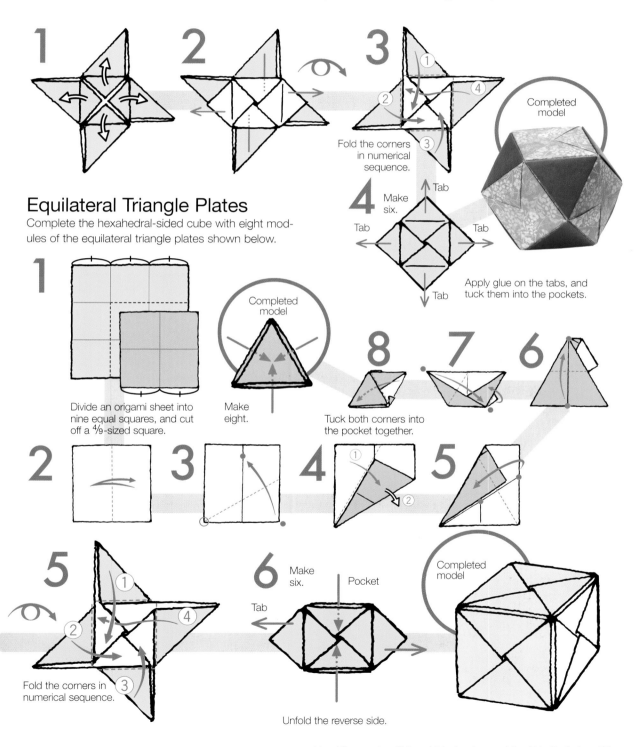

1

2

3

Fold the corners in numerical sequence.

Completed model

4 Make six.

Tab

Tab

Tab

Tab

Apply glue on the tabs, and tuck them into the pockets.

Equilateral Triangle Plates

Complete the hexahedral-sided cube with eight modules of the equilateral triangle plates shown below.

1

Divide an origami sheet into nine equal squares, and cut off a $\frac{4}{9}$-sized square.

Completed model

Make eight.

8

7

6

Tuck both corners into the pocket together.

2

3

4

5

5

Fold the corners in numerical sequence.

6 Make six.

Pocket

Tab

Completed model

Unfold the reverse side.

Assembling the *Tamatebako* with Hexagonal Sides

Tuck the tabs into the pockets of the triangle.

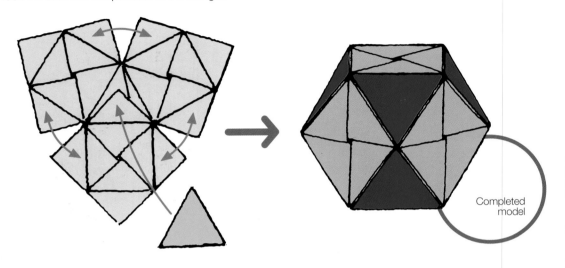

Completed model

How I Rediscovered the *Tamatebako*

Let me tell you a little more about how I came to rediscover the *Tamatebako*.

As far as I know, the oldest publication in which the *Tamatebako* appears is *Ranma-Zushiki* in 1734. Its next appearance, according to Satoshi Takagi, was in a drawing of the *Tamatebako*, the *Komosou*, and the Frog in *On'na-you Kyokun Ehon Hana-no-en* (*Instructional Picture Book for Women*) in 1752.

In 1849, the *Tamatebako* appeared on the outside cover of a picture book, *Jiraiya Gouketsu Tan* (*A Heroic Story of Jiraiya*) by Kunisada Utagawa. In the summer of 2001, a woodblock print of the hexahedral-sided *Tamatebako* used as a container was exhibited in the Edo Ukiyo-e Museum in Tokyo. The hexahedral-sided cube was also shown in a monthly magazine for children called *Sho-kokumin* (*Ordinary Citizens*) published in 1894.

In 1933, I found that Isao Honda introduced both the hexahedral and the regular *Tamatebako* in his publication, *Origami* (Kogyo Tosho K.K.) Also, as I described on page 39, in *Paper Toy Making* (First Edition, 1937), the *Tamatebako* is presented as the Stamp Box.

The most recent appearance of the hexahedral *Tamatebako* was Honda's book, *Origami Nippon: Honda Origami Studio* (1970), in which the *Tamatebako* is presented as Kakugata *Kumiawase-Bako*, or a box assembled with parts. However, I did not pay much attention to this work, because in those days, I stubbornly believed that origami should not require cutting or pasting (Honda's box required cutting). Thus, after all these twists and turns, I finally rediscovered the masterpiece.

Interpretations Make Origami More Fun

Part of the fun of origami is how you interpret the models. Origami models, of course, are open to a wide range of interpretations. For example, the model known as the *Hakama*, which is like a kilt or pleated skirt in Japan, is called Pants in Europe. Both interpretations are not so different because both represent clothes. When I see the Sleeve-Waving *Yakko* described as Rider (*Shogun*) on page 44 or Monkey on page 45, I think it's amazing.

Consider an interesting interpretation of the Monkey. Turn it around and make it sway to music. Doesn't it look like an opera singer? Can you picture a master tenor singing his heart out?

Karasu Tengu
(Crowlike, Long-Nosed Goblin)

Eye Lantern

"Volare!"

"Bravo! Bravo!"

Fun with Decorative Models

So far, I have described my personal study of *Ranma-Zushiki*. Now, let's enjoy folding some variations of the *Tamatebako*. Think about the development of forms from *Itoire* to *Menko*, from third-fold Pinwheels to quarter-fold Pinwheels, and from Froebel's basic forms to the *Tamatebako*. This exercise is an evolution from planes to three-dimensional shapes, from basic forms to beautiful flower boxes, leading finally to decorative cubes.

Let's try folding some flower boxes and decorative cubes. Although these models are merely variations of the *Tamatebako* and the *Tamatebako* with Hexaheral Sides, their beauty never fails to delight.

Flower Box

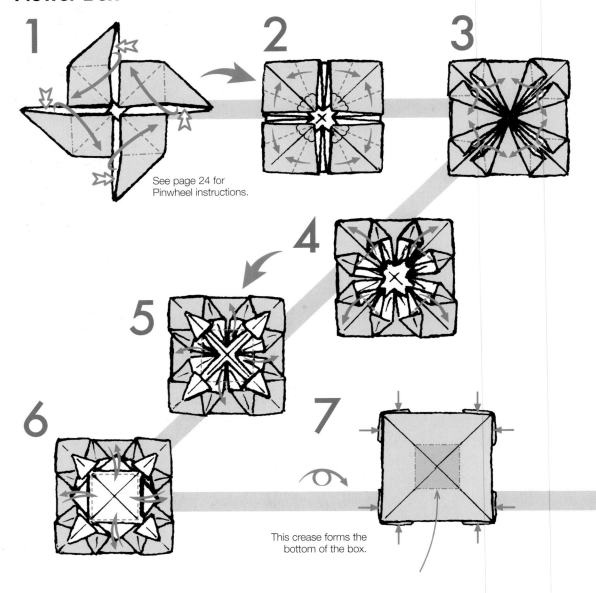

See page 24 for Pinwheel instructions.

This crease forms the bottom of the box.

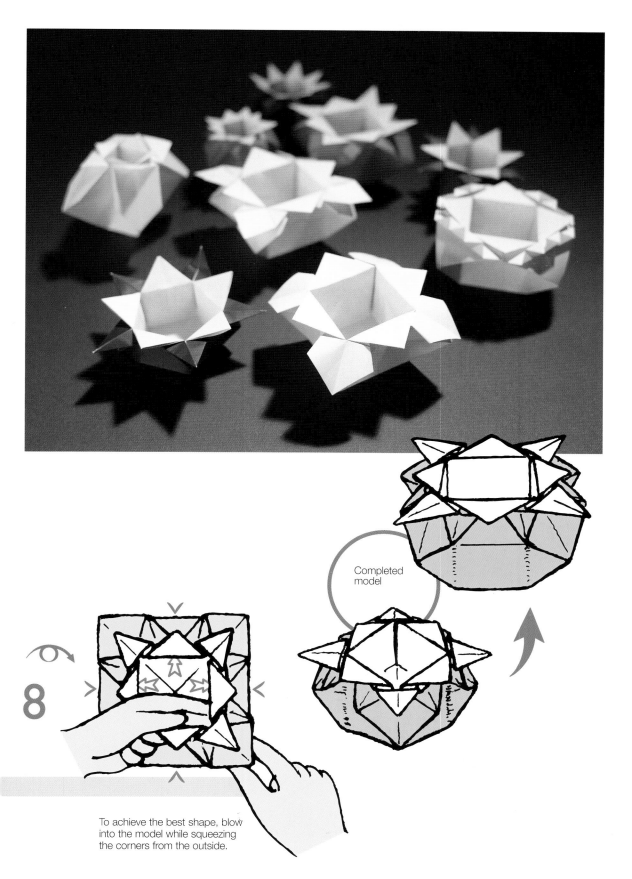

8

Completed model

To achieve the best shape, blow into the model while squeezing the corners from the outside.

Origami Flower Garden

Origami is an endlessly evolving art. Use today's newly invented decorative models to turn your desk into an origami flower garden. Consider Froebel's basic forms (page 43) the seeds of these flowers. With just a twist, you can fold the beautiful designs of the basic forms into stunning containers. Most basic forms can be turned into decorative cubes by using tabs that are one-eighth the size of a standard sheet of origami paper. Try folding the cubes with sheets shaped like equilateral triangles, regular pentagons, hexagons, octagons, and other regular polygons—you will see what is possible.

Decorative Cube

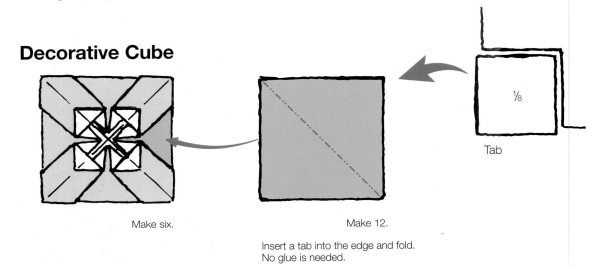

Make six.

⅛

Tab

Make 12.

Insert a tab into the edge and fold. No glue is needed.

Basic Forms

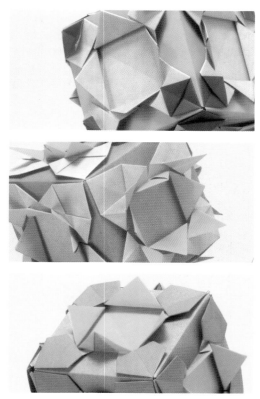

Beautiful Flower Boxes of All Shapes

In observing that most of Froebel's basic forms can be turned into attractive flower boxes, we can see how they change form when we fold them with differently shaped bases. The models look so different that it is hard to believe they are all folded in the same manner.

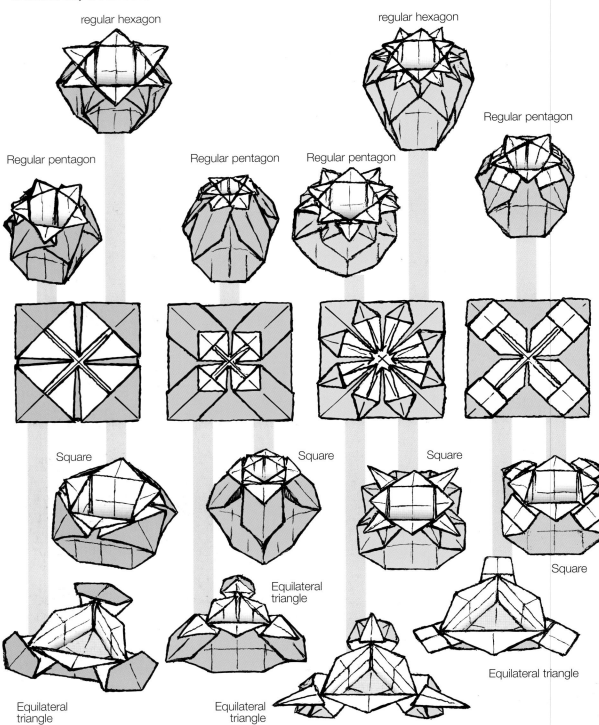

regular hexagon

regular hexagon

Regular pentagon

Regular pentagon

Regular pentagon

Regular pentagon

Regular pentagon

Square

Square

Square

Square

Equilateral triangle

Equilateral triangle

Equilateral triangle

Equilateral triangle

Equilateral triangle

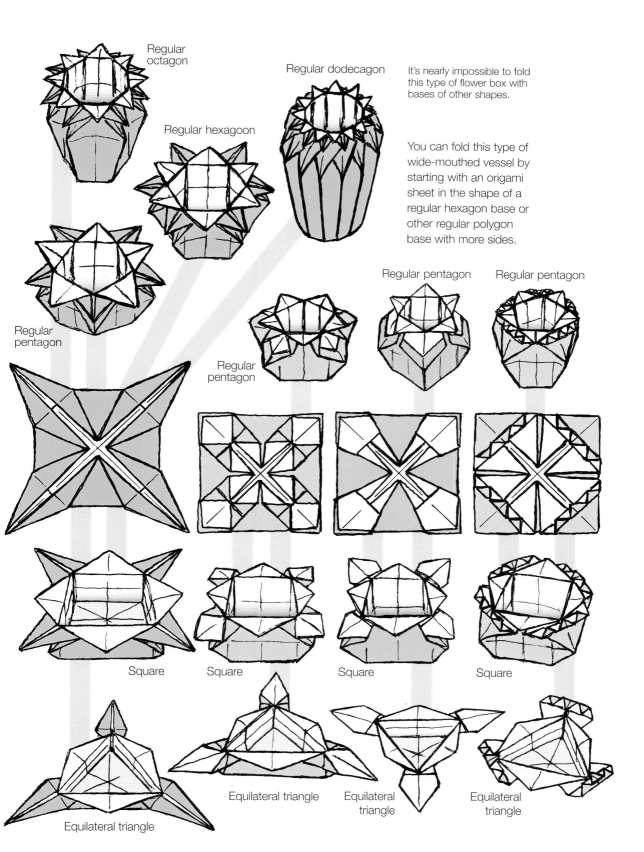

Regular
octagon

Regular hexagoon

Regular dodecagon

It's nearly impossible to fold
this type of flower box with
bases of other shapes.

You can fold this type of
wide-mouthed vessel by
starting with an origami
sheet in the shape of a
regular hexagon base or
other regular polygon
base with more sides.

Regular
pentagon

Regular
pentagon

Regular pentagon

Regular pentagon

Square

Square

Square

Square

Equilateral triangle

Equilateral triangle

Equilateral
triangle

Equilateral
triangle

Equilateral triangle

Making Regular Polygons for Pinwheel Models

Equilateral Triangle

 **1**   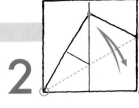 **2**   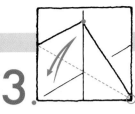 **3**    **4**

Square

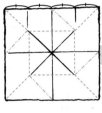 **1**

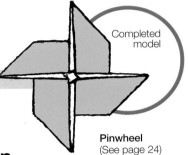

Completed model

Pinwheel
(See page 24)

5

Regular Pentagon

1    **2**    **3**    **4**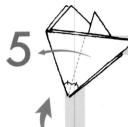

Make a very short crease in the upper layer only.

Note the difference in folding angles.

Regular Hexagon

1    **2**    **3**    **4**

Make a longer crease than in the Regular Pentagon model.

60°

Regular Octagon

1 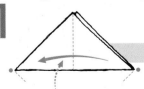   **2**    **3**    **4**

Open and press.

Regular Dodecagon

Start with five octagons, as folded above.

Make a longer crease than for the Regular Octagon model.

1   **2**  30°   **3**    **4**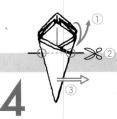

①
②
③

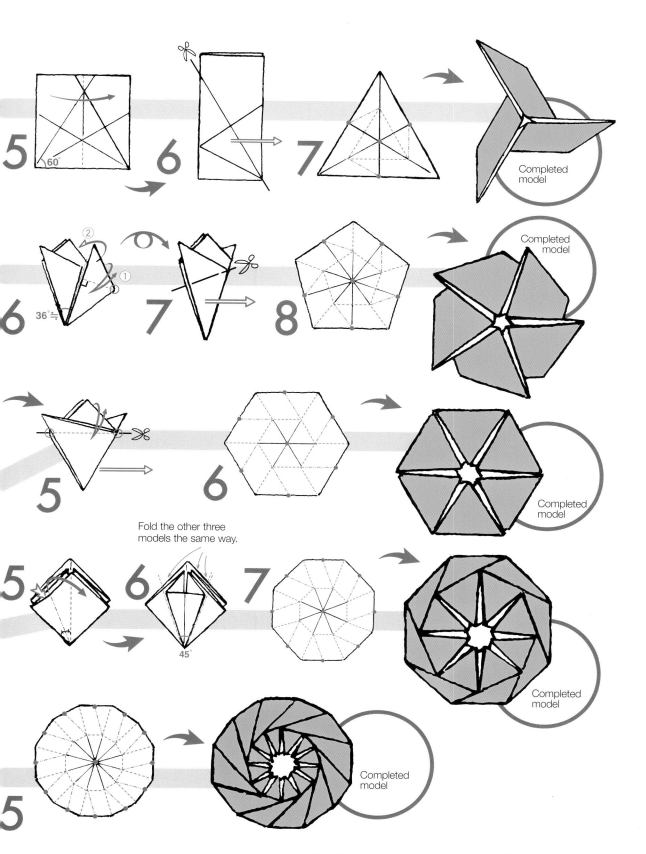

5 60°

6

7

Completed model

6 36°≒

7

8

Completed model

5

6

Completed model

Fold the other three models the same way.

5

6 45°

7

Completed model

5

Completed model

Making a Kaleidoscope from an Equilateral Triangle Base

You create the basic forms by folding various polygon bases. If you fold them with equilateral triangle bases, you will be treated to a kaleidoscope of dazzling triangular patterns.

SLIDESHOW

Kaleidoscope

Making Snowflakes
from a Regular Hexagon Base

If you put together six triangles, you make a hexagon. When we fold the basic
forms using hexagon bases, we get snowflakes. These delicate patterns are the
result of the standard origami sheets being white on one side.

Snowflakes

Hints on Making Snowflakes

Try making your own patterns for snowflakes. Two basic folding techniques are diagramed below. Make as many regular hexagon bases as you like, and explore an endless array of new patterns.

Making a Regular Hexagon Base

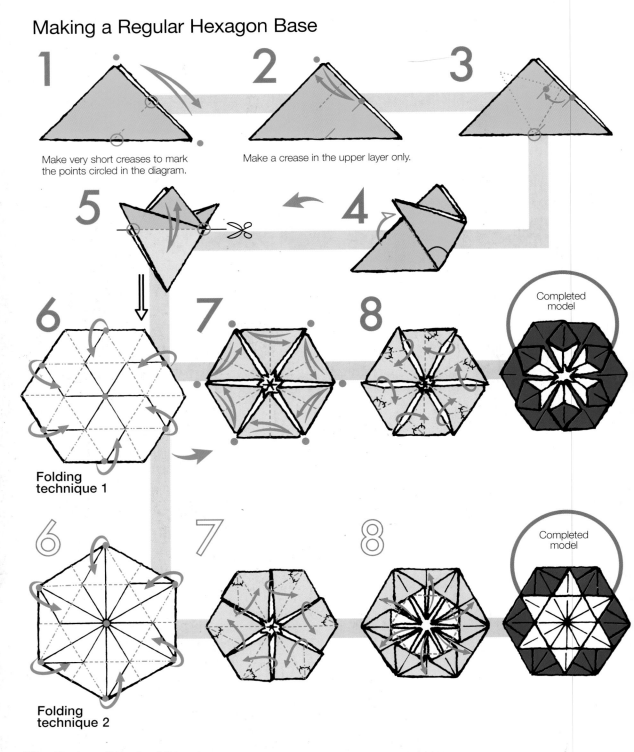

1 Make very short creases to mark the points circled in the diagram.

2 Make a crease in the upper layer only.

3

4

5

6 Folding technique 1

7

8

Completed model

6 Folding technique 2

7

8

Completed model

Intriguing Origami Cubes Chapter 3

The *Beniire* Cube

It is surprising to learn that the cube was folded 270 years ago (see Chapter 2 for more details). Even more surprising, however, is that multiple sheets of paper were used to form the three-dimensional figure. Today we call such origami models "unit origami" (in Japan) or modular origami (in the West). Ohoka's cube is one of the earliest predecessors of modular origami.

This project illustrates cubes that not only are solid but have interesting faces and functions as well. These are models that you can enjoy both by folding and by displaying. The first type of cube is made from a *Beniire* base, the traditional origami work of the Maeda family. Two-sheet, three-sheet, and six-sheet modular origami can be developed from nearly identical forms.

The origami cube has been a lifelong pursuit of mine. I have collected more than 500 origami cubes, including my own designs. In my opinion, the *Tamatebako* is one of the ten-best cubes ever created. Yet, I have been trying to make an even better cube myself. I'll let you be the judge of which cube is the best.

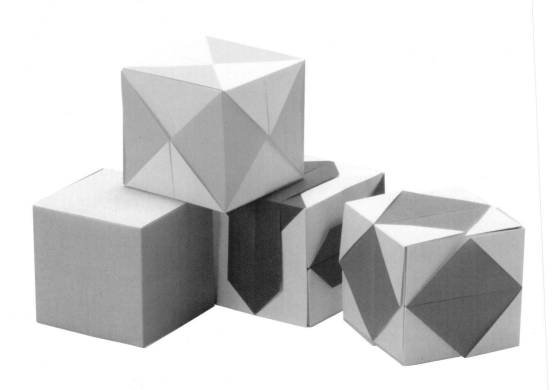

Beniire Cube Made with Two Modules

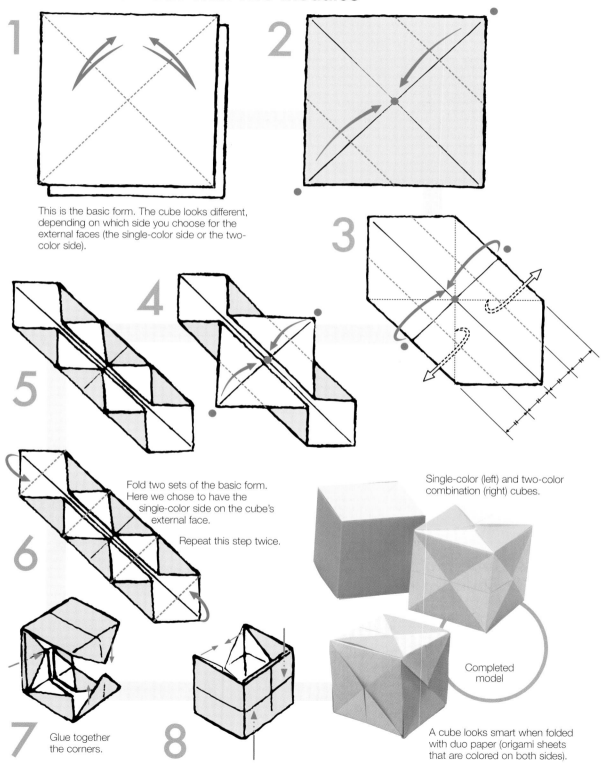

1

2

This is the basic form. The cube looks different, depending on which side you choose for the external faces (the single-color side or the two-color side).

3

4

5

6

Fold two sets of the basic form. Here we chose to have the single-color side on the cube's external face.

Repeat this step twice.

Single-color (left) and two-color combination (right) cubes.

Completed model

7 Glue together the corners.

8

A cube looks smart when folded with duo paper (origami sheets that are colored on both sides).

Beniire Cube Made with Three Modules

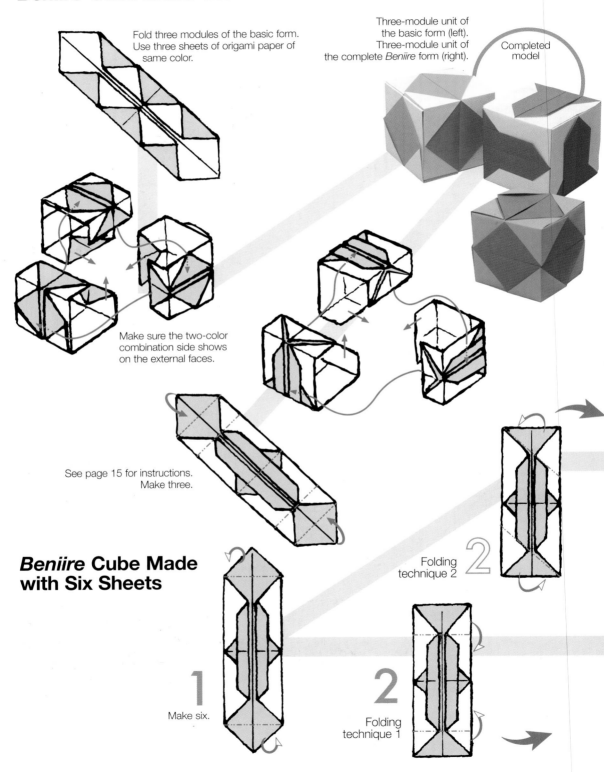

Fold three modules of the basic form. Use three sheets of origami paper of same color.

Three-module unit of the basic form (left). Three-module unit of the complete *Beniire* form (right).

Completed model

Make sure the two-color combination side shows on the external faces.

See page 15 for instructions. Make three.

Beniire Cube Made with Six Sheets

Make six.

Folding technique 2

Folding technique 1

Four Elements of the Cube

A cube has the following four geometric elements:
1. Six square faces
2. Twelve edges of equal length
3. Eight points.
4. One central point.

When you try to fold a new type of cube, these elements will guide you to find the correct folding technique. Although focusing on a single central point may make the model more complicated, the other three elements are helpful. Remember the numeral pattern of six, twelve, and eight, and you will see them appear when you try to fold the cube.

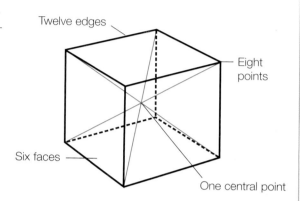

Twelve edges

Eight points

Six faces

One central point

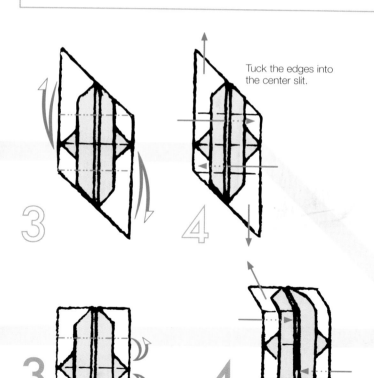

Tuck the edges into the center slit.

3

4

3

4

Tuck the edges under the colored sides.

The cube on the left was created using folding technique 1 whereas the one on the right was made using folding technique 2. Both cubes were folded with duo origami sheets.

Completed model

Fun with a Four-Dimensional Cube

You can make a two-dimensional form from of a three-dimensional form by adding two folding lines to a set of two cubes to make a *Beniire* (introduced on page 75). Here's an idea: Try putting several cubes that are pasted together into a box! That's the mysterious four-dimensional cube!

Four-Dimensional Cube

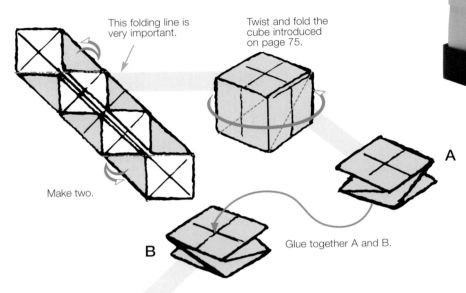

This folding line is very important.

Twist and fold the cube introduced on page 75.

A

Make two.

B

Glue together A and B.

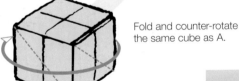

Fold and counter-rotate the same cube as A.

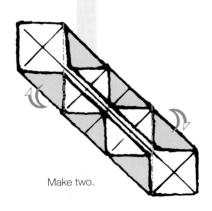

Make two.

Put 6 to 16 A and B cubes alternately between two traditional *masu* (open-ended boxes), and enjoy opening them up.

Four-Dimensional Cube Box (*Masu* Box)

Now try making a four-dimensional cube "box" from of traditional *masu* boxes (combination of big and small).

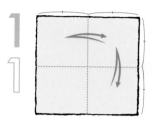

1

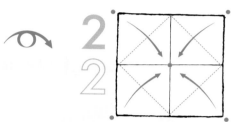

2

Make a paper square that is ⅜" (1 cm) larger than the one used for the four-dimensional cube.

3

Pay attention to the difference between the "lid" and "body" of the box.

3

Big (lid)

Fold and leave a ⅕" (4 mm) space between the edges of the folded paper. Fold and leave no space between papers.

Small (body)

4 4

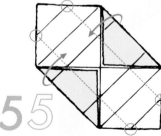

5 5

Complete the process by gluing both edges of the four-dimensional cube (shown on page 78) to A and B, which have already been glued together as a box.

6 6

Make the two sides stand up perpendicular to the base. The lid should have a wider gap in the middle.

7 7

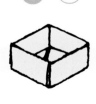

8 8

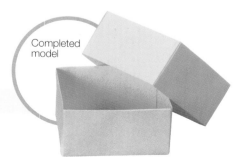

Completed model

What Is Modular Origami?

Most origami fans have heard of modular, or unit, origami. The terms simply mean an origami assembly. To make a modular origami model, you first must divide a solid model into equal parts. Then, make the origami modules (or units), and put them together to form the assembly. By using a number of modules for an assembly, you can more easily make a figure than by folding a single sheet. From this point of view, we may call the 270-year-old *Tamatebako* in *Ranma-Zushiki* an example of modular origami. This chapter will show you several modular origami models.

Cube Puzzle, Part 1

You can see that modular origami pieces, particularly cubes, are quite puzzling when you try to assemble them, though the modules themselves are easy to fold. The following pages will show you some assembly puzzles for modular cubes. The first is a six-module cube. Try to discover how to assemble the cube shown below using the modules. In this example, each module assumes two edges of the cube. Therefore, we need six modules to cover all edges of the cube, expressed in the formula, 12/2=6. In some six-module cubes, each module makes up a face of the cube, instead of two edges.

Six-Sheet Modular Cube

How do you assemble this cube with the modules below?

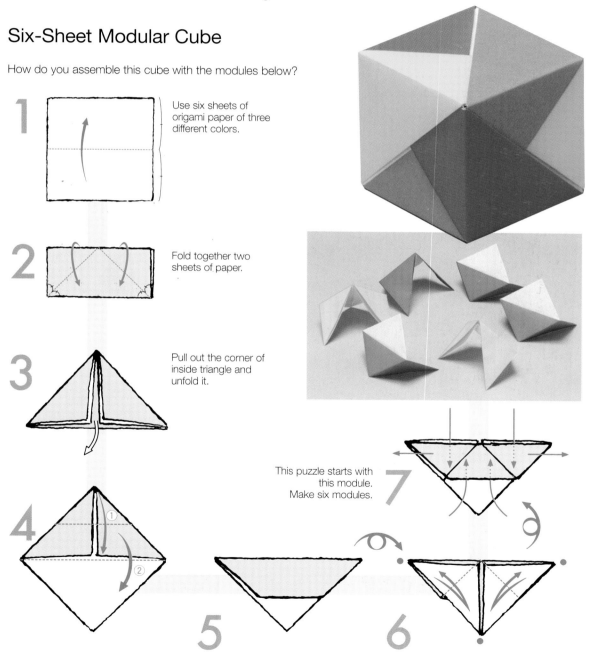

1 Use six sheets of origami paper of three different colors.

2 Fold together two sheets of paper.

3 Pull out the corner of inside triangle and unfold it.

4

5

6

7 This puzzle starts with this module. Make six modules.

Usually, the modules of a modular origami model have the same number of tabs and pockets. However, the type shown in the Cube Puzzle, Part 1 has more pockets than tabs, as shown below. This is why the assembly method becomes a puzzle. Though the answer is shown below, it is still hard to understand how to assemble it at a glance. When you can locate three colors symmetrically and fit the modules so firmly together that it will not come apart when lifted, you have solved the puzzle.

How to Assemble the Cube (Solution)

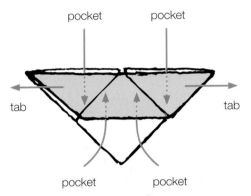

pocket   pocket

tab   tab

pocket   pocket

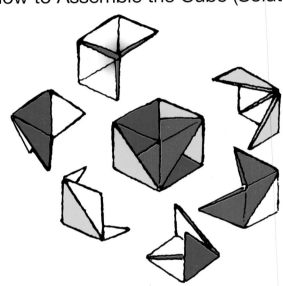

Cube Puzzle, Part 2

Here is the second puzzle for an eight-module cube. The number eight may tell you that the units in this cube take all eight points (see page 77). Surprisingly, such a cube is rarely achieved, because it is difficult to match the units' points exactly with the cube's points during assembly. This cube comes apart easily, but you can turn this disadvantage into an advantage. Use this model to make an enjoyable origami attraction or an "origami firework." See the next page for details.

Eight-Sheet Modular Cube

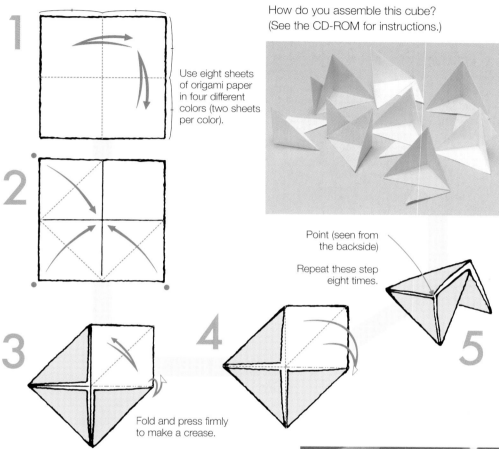

1 Use eight sheets of origami paper in four different colors (two sheets per color).

2

How do you assemble this cube?
(See the CD-ROM for instructions.)

Point (seen from the backside)

Repeat these step eight times.

3 Fold and press firmly to make a crease.

4

5

Origami Fireworks

When you slap the cube after tossing it in the air, it bursts apart like a firework display and all the pieces come fluttering down. This amazing idea for origami fireworks came from Paulo Taborda Barreto, a Portuguese friend who lives in Holland. He showed me a modular cube assembly made of twelve modules and featuring eight points that are inside-folded to hold the assembly together. This folding technique requires close attention. My own version is more easily assembled.

MOVIE

The Double Cube (A Seven-Sheet Assembly)

Actually, the number seven has nothing to do with the actual elements of a cube, a fact that makes this seven-sheet assembly a puzzle in itself. In short, the seven-sheet assembly shown here is two three-module cubes connected with one module. This origami toy is simple but entertaining for children because of how it changes shape. Enjoy this origami in motion.

Double Cube

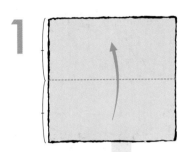

Use seven sheets of origami paper; three sheets of one color, three sheets of another color, and one sheet in a third color. Make two sets.

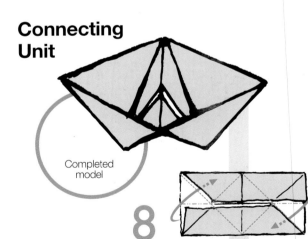

Fold two modules of the Lotus (see page 90 for instructions) with six sheets of origami paper (three sheets of the same color for each module) and a connecting unit with one sheet (of the third color).

Make 2 sets.

Connecting Unit

Completed model

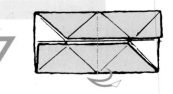

Tuck the corner into the pocket, lifting up the top layer. Repeat this step for each module.

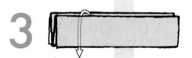

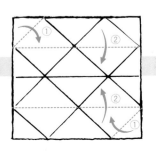

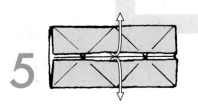

How to Assemble

Connecting Unit

Open the connecting unit's center slit, and tuck a corner of each triangle into it.

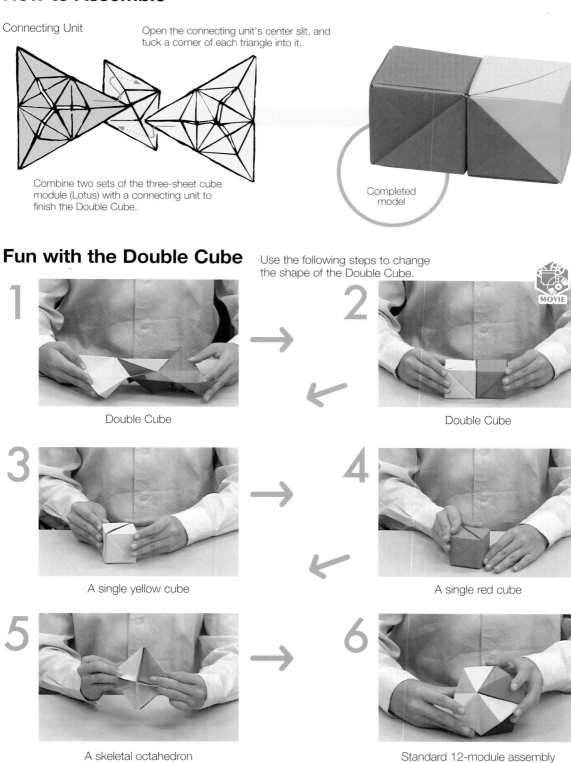

Combine two sets of the three-sheet cube module (Lotus) with a connecting unit to finish the Double Cube.

Completed model

Fun with the Double Cube

Use the following steps to change the shape of the Double Cube.

MOVIE

1 → Double Cube

2 Double Cube

3 A single yellow cube →

4 A single red cube

5 A skeletal octahedron →

6 Standard 12-module assembly

Regular Tetrahedrons and Cubes

The steps in this section show how to make a regular tetrahedron. Both this tetrahedron and the skeletal octahedron (or the Double Cube turned inside out) consist of equally sized equilateral triangles. In addition to these shapes, you can make other regular polyhedrons, including a regular dodecahedron (three regular pentagons at each corner) and a regular hexahedron or a cube.

Let's look at the geometric relationship between a regular tetrahedron and a cube, both of which consist of equilateral triangles. A modular origami model of the cube containing a tetrahedron follows.

Tetrahedron

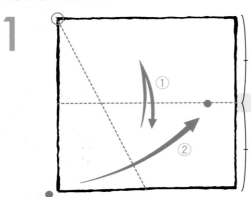

Pay attention to • when you fold the bottom-left corner in step 2.

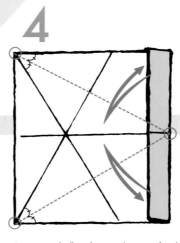

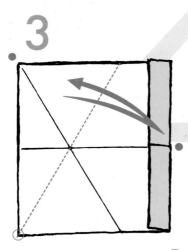

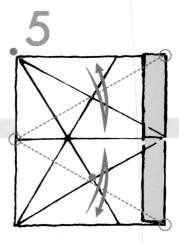

These steps are challenging, so try your best.

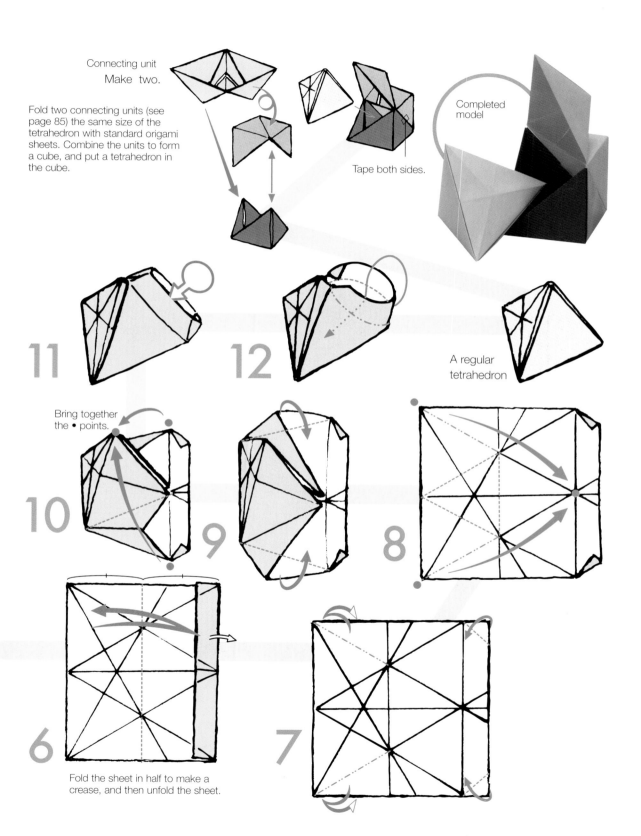

Connecting unit
Make two.

Fold two connecting units (see page 85) the same size of the tetrahedron with standard origami sheets. Combine the units to form a cube, and put a tetrahedron in the cube.

Tape both sides.

Completed model

11

12

A regular tetrahedron

Bring together the • points.

10

9

8

6

Fold the sheet in half to make a crease, and then unfold the sheet.

7

Buddha Statue

This statue of Buddha seated in a three-module Lotus Flower cube is made using the traditional *Yakko* and *Hakama* models shown in Chapter 1. In addition, you can create a decorative stand, a lotus pedestal, a halo, and a seat for Buddha. Though this piece is challenging, try your best—you will be rewarded with an origami good-luck charm.

Buddha Statue

This statue is a six-module origami assembly.

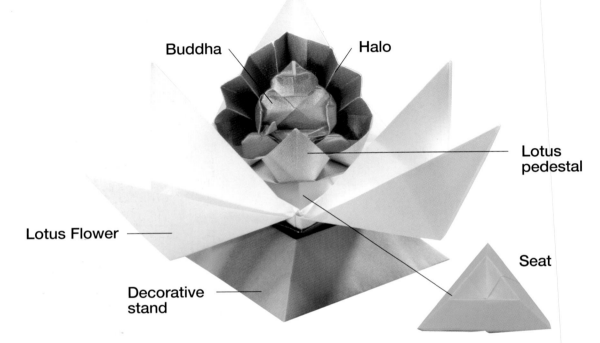

Buddha · Halo

Lotus pedestal

Lotus Flower

Seat

Decorative stand

Origami Paper Sizes for Each Module

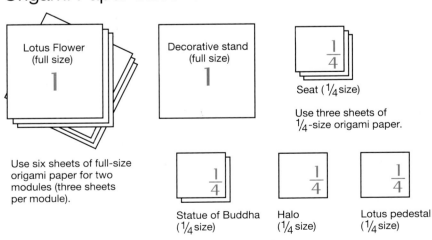

Lotus Flower (full size)

1

Use six sheets of full-size origami paper for two modules (three sheets per module).

Decorative stand (full size)

1

Seat ($\frac{1}{4}$ size)

$\frac{1}{4}$

Use three sheets of $\frac{1}{4}$-size origami paper.

Statue of Buddha ($\frac{1}{4}$ size)

$\frac{1}{4}$

Halo ($\frac{1}{4}$ size)

$\frac{1}{4}$

Lotus pedestal ($\frac{1}{4}$ size)

$\frac{1}{4}$

Use two sheets of $\frac{1}{4}$ size origami paper.

Decorative Stand

Fold the base first. You can also use this base to display other modular origami models, such as cubes. Fold it with a regular-size sheet of origami paper.

Completed model

1

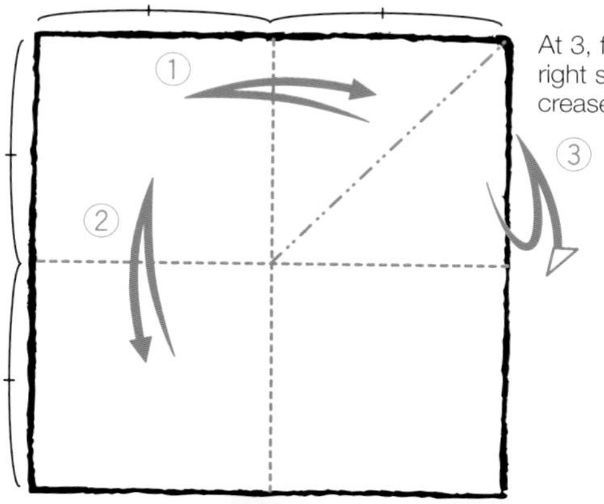

At 3, fold only the top-right square to make a crease.

2

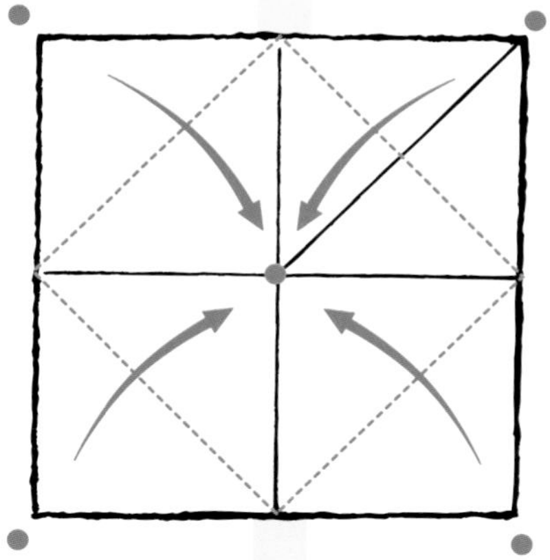

3

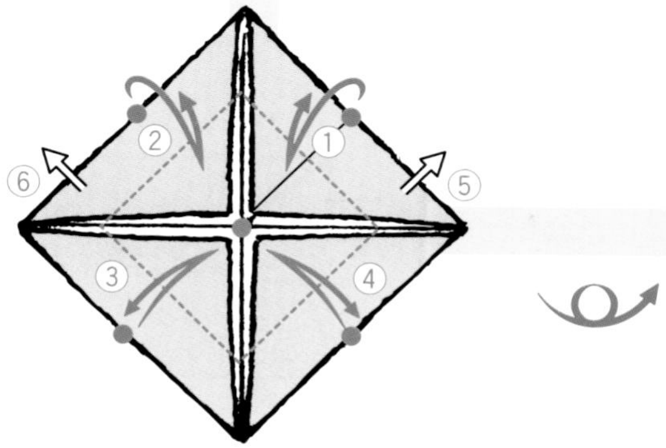

6

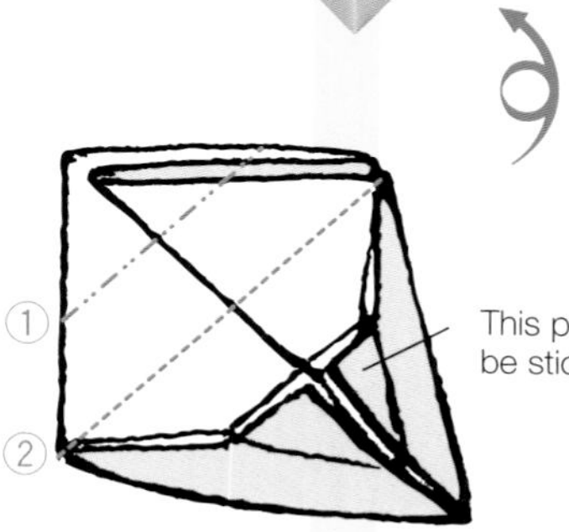

This part should be sticking out.

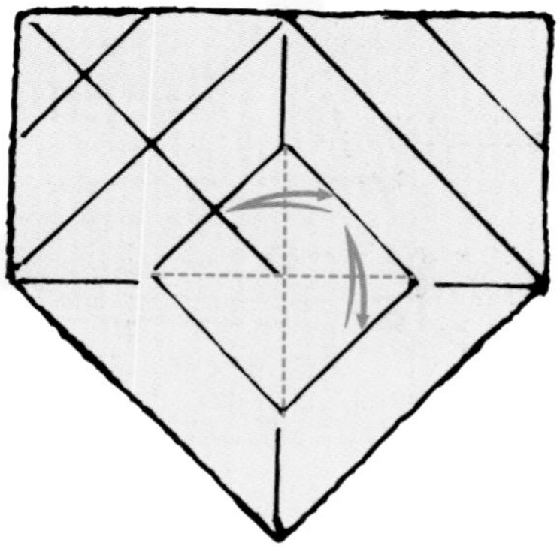

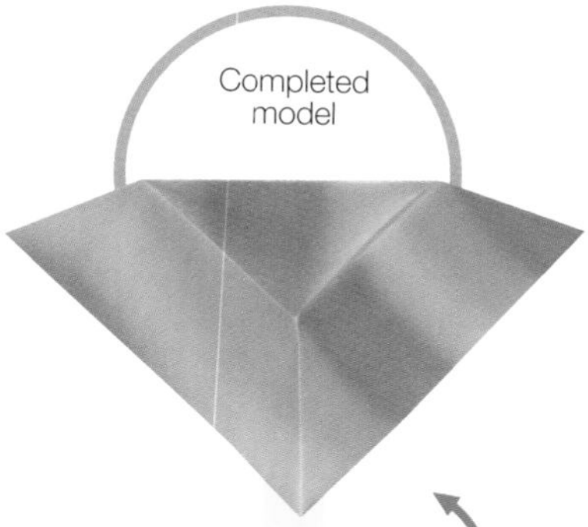

5

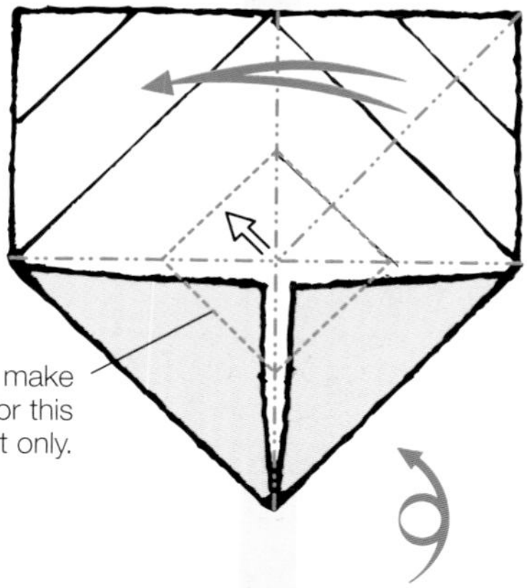

Fold to make creases for this part only.

4

Lotus Flower Made from Three Cubes

The Lotus Flower is a three-module cube, just like the cube shown on page 76, but its modules are already three-dimensional. Put two Lotus Flowers together to make the larger one on which the Buddha will sit.

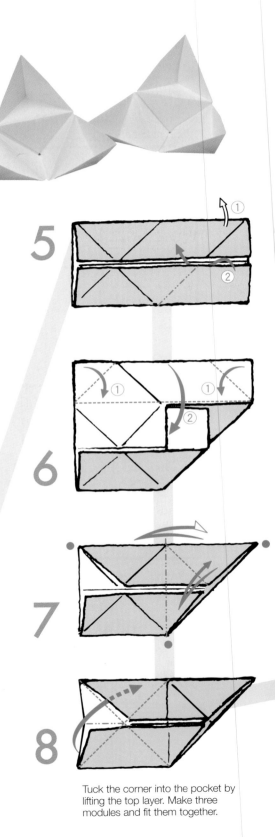

Use six sheets of regular origami paper (three sheets per set).

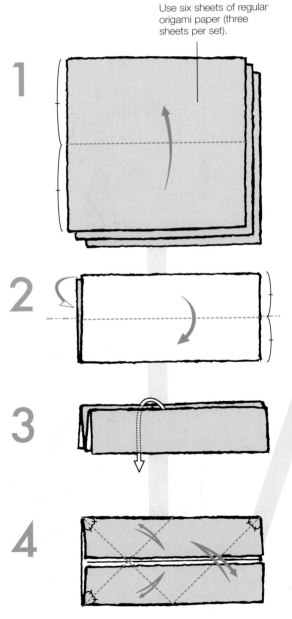

1

2

3

4

Fold to make a crease, bringing corner points to outer edges.

5
① ②

6
① ① ②

7

8

Tuck the corner into the pocket by lifting the top layer. Make three modules and fit them together.

Pedestal

Use three sheets of ¼-size origami paper to make the pedestal that will be Buddha's seat.

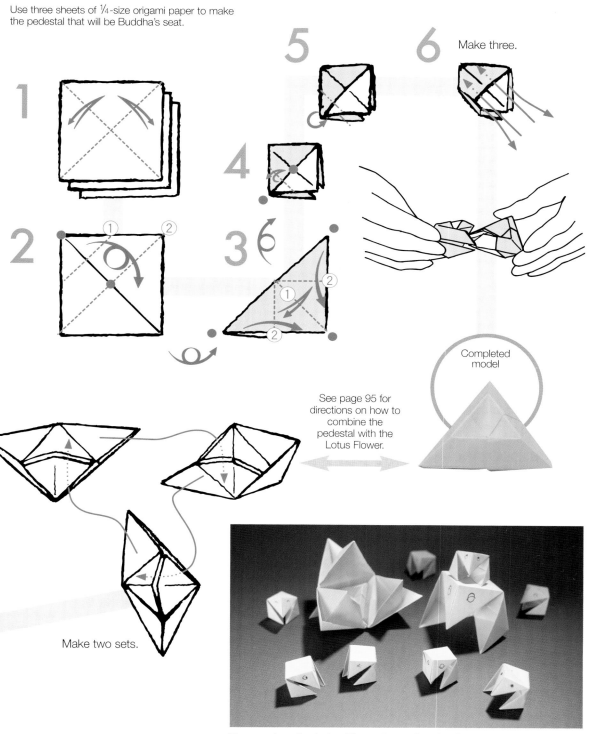

5

6 Make three.

1

4

2

3

See page 95 for directions on how to combine the pedestal with the Lotus Flower.

Completed model

Make two sets.

You can turn the Lotus Flower into a frog family.

Buddha Statue with Halo and Lotus Pedestal

Now you'll make the Buddha statue using a combination of *Yakko* and *Hakama* origami. You need four sheets of ¼-size origami paper: two sheets for the statue, one sheet for the halo, and one sheet for the lotus pedestal. Cut a sheet of full-size origami paper into four equal squares to make the sheets.

Buddha

1

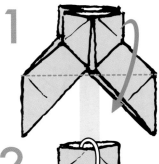

2

Pull back the face part.

3

Upper body (Sleeve-Waving *Yakko*)

4

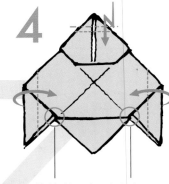

Fold side edges in to here.

5

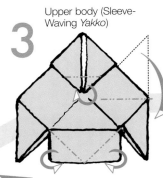

① ②

Tuck the point into the pocket.

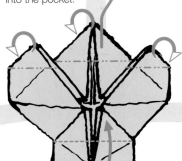

6

Fold only the bottom layer, leaving the face untouched.

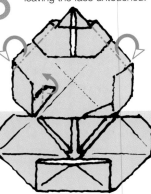

Lower body (*Hakama*)

Fold the top layer to the reverse side.

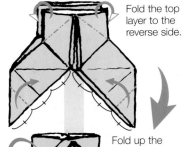

Fold up the lower points by a third.

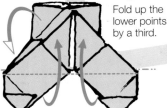

Halo

Use a ¼-size sheet of origami paper.

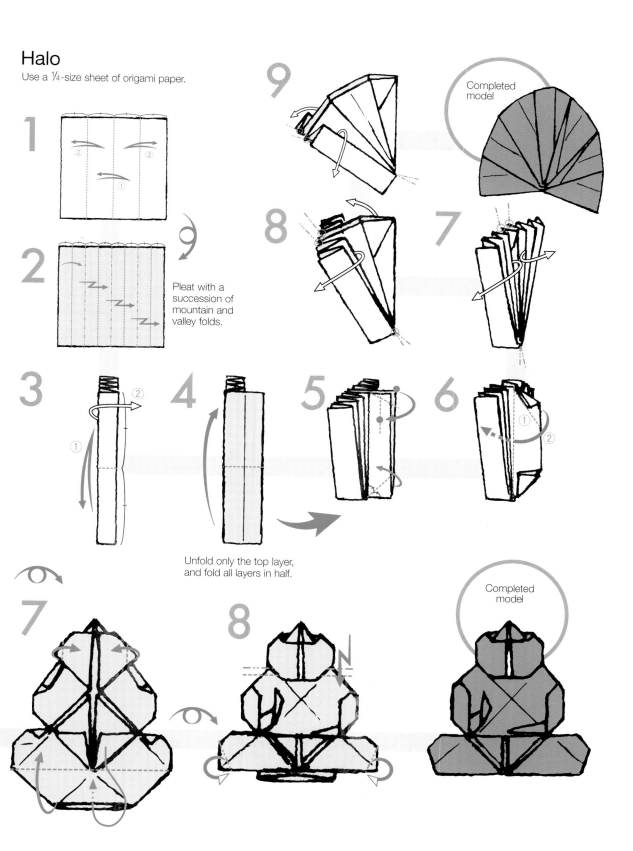

Pleat with a
succession of
mountain and
valley folds.

Unfold only the top layer,
and fold all layers in half.

Completed
model

Completed
model

Lotus Pedestal

Use a ¼-size sheet of origami paper.

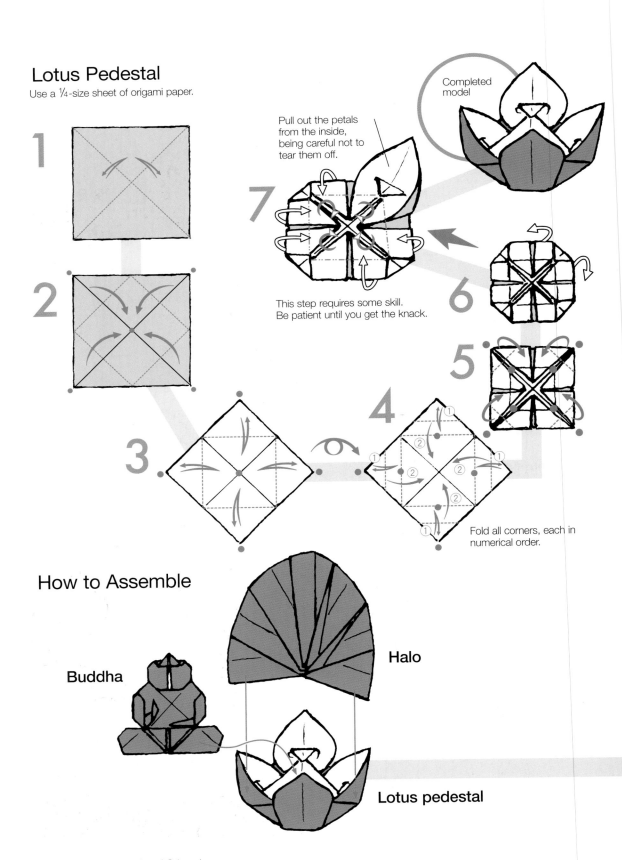

1

2

3

4

Fold all corners, each in numerical order.

5

6

7

Pull out the petals from the inside, being careful not to tear them off.

This step requires some skill. Be patient until you get the knack.

Completed model

How to Assemble

Buddha

Halo

Lotus pedestal

Other Uses for the *Yakko* Method

Buddha is not all the *Yakko* character makes. You can also use the *Yakko* base to make a six-module polyhedron assembly.

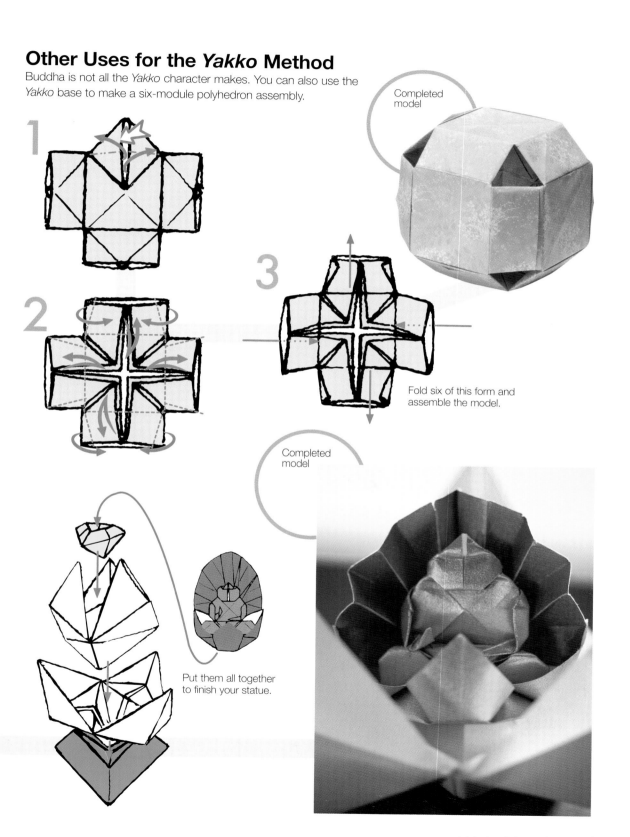

1

2

3

Fold six of this form and assemble the model.

Completed model

Completed model

Put them all together to finish your statue.

The Magic Cube:
An Embodiment of Modular Origami

To close this chapter on intriguing cubes, you will make a playful, puzzlelike cube using the following materials:

three sheets of blue origami paper

one sheet of orange origami paper

one sheet of red origami paper (cut it into halves to use either half)

With these sheets, you will make five modules: A, B, C, D, and E. Like magic, this cube changes into various forms, so the project is named the "Magic Cube." Have fun folding it.

Magic Cube

Start with three sheets of blue origami paper

1

2

See page 90 for instructions up to step 7.

3

Make a pyramid in the triangle pocket.

A

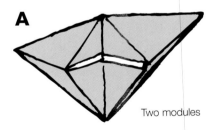

Two modules

To make A, refer to page 90. After you have completed A and B, fit the three modules together using the same method you used for the Lotus Flower model.

B

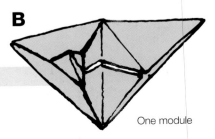

One module

Start with one sheet of orange origami paper.

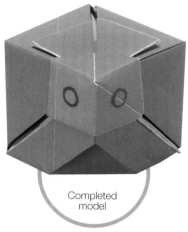

C

This is a regular tetrahedron. See page 87 for instructions.

Completed model

The cube looks like this when completed. Don't give up until you can do it.

Start with one sheet of red origami paper.
Cut the sheet in half and use each half to make modules D and E (instructions for E are on the next page).

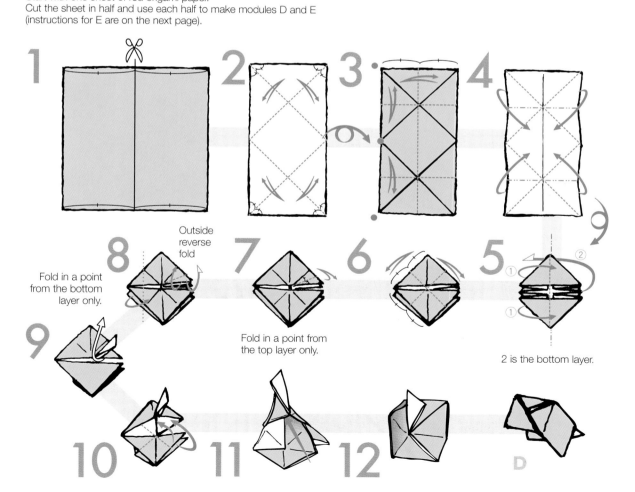

1

2

3

4

5

① ② ①

2 is the bottom layer.

6

7

Fold in a point from the top layer only.

8

Outside reverse fold

Fold in a point from the bottom layer only.

9

10

11

12

D

Make module E with the other half of the red sheet.

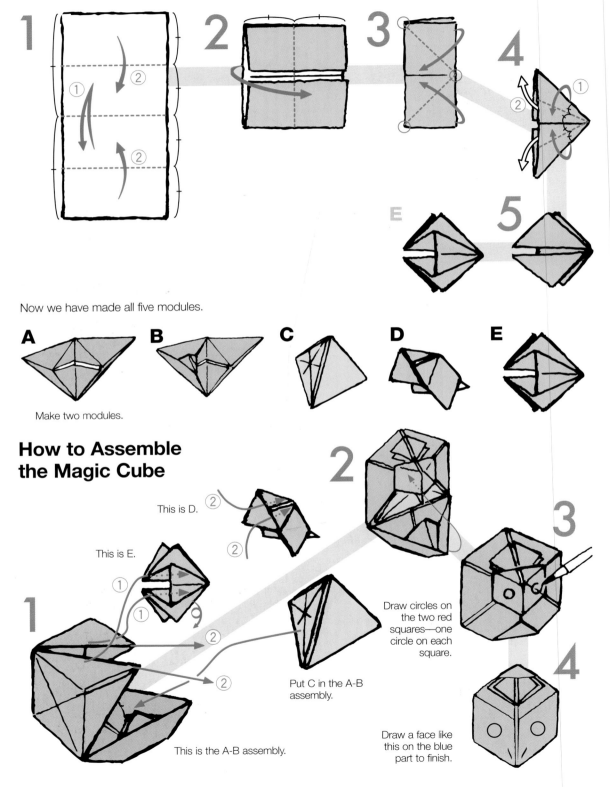

Now we have made all five modules.

A **B** **C** **D** **E**

Make two modules.

How to Assemble the Magic Cube

This is D.

This is E.

This is the A-B assembly.

Put C in the A-B assembly.

Draw circles on the two red squares—one circle on each square.

Draw a face like this on the blue part to finish.

How to Play with the Magic Cube

Now you can enjoy the magic.
See what you can turn the model into.

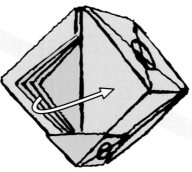

First it's a red sailboat.

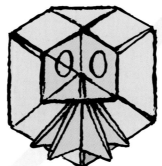

Now, it's an octopus.

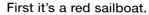

No, it's a goldfish.

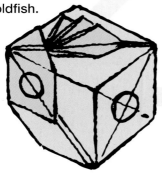

Well, no, it's actually a
big-mouthed angelfish!

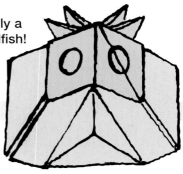

Continued on the next page.

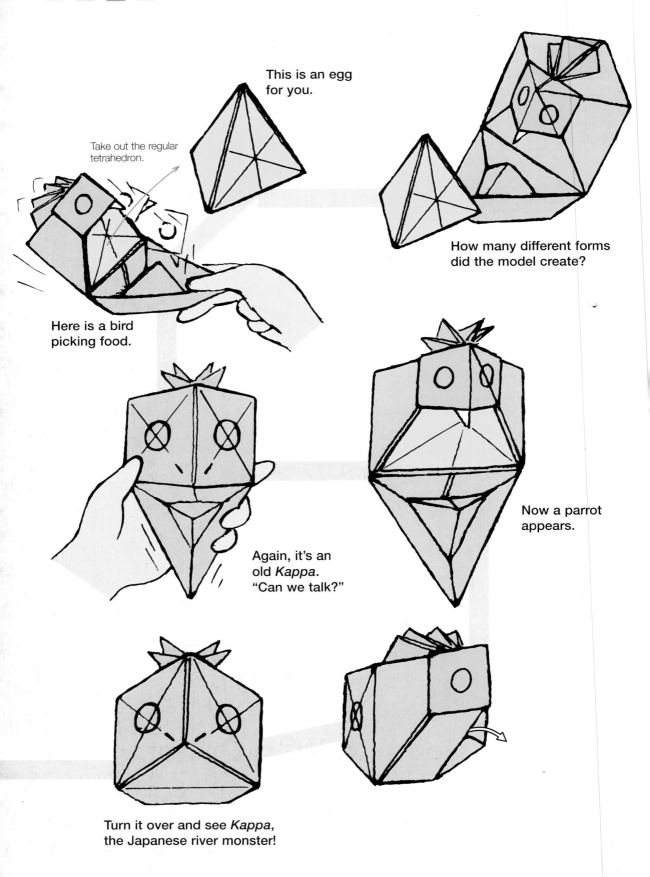

This is an egg for you.

Take out the regular tetrahedron.

Here is a bird picking food.

How many different forms did the model create?

Again, it's an old *Kappa*. "Can we talk?"

Now a parrot appears.

Turn it over and see *Kappa*, the Japanese river monster!

Cube Art: Painting With Origami

Chapter 4

Painting Pictures with Origami

This chapter will teach you "cube art," my latest origami invention. As mentioned in Chapter 1, an important feature of origami paper—sheets of paper exclusively designed for origami folding—is that it is colored on one side and white on the other. This type of paper did not exist in Japan in the Edo or early Meiji periods. In the Edo period, origami models were folded with paper that had the same pattern on both sides. Today, thanks to developments in printing and papermaking, we can choose from a wide variety of beautiful origami paper of the highest quality—paper that people of the Edo or Meiji periods could never have imagined.

When I first became interested in the two-sided nature of origami paper, I decided to use the different patterns to paint a picture on a square canvas, tucking the edges or tabs into pockets at the cube's corners. I named the work "cube art."

I believe I am still the only origami folder who makes cube art. I hope you will join me in pursuing this fascinating origami application and become an enthusiastic artist of it yourself.

As you master various folding techniques, you can create your own art. Let me show you some of my favorite models from my collection of more than 200 works of cube art. Use these examples to develop your own technique.

Cube Art

In this new form of origami art, you use both sides of a sheet of origami paper to "paint" a picture. The picture you create will appear on a cube's face; hence, I call it cube art.

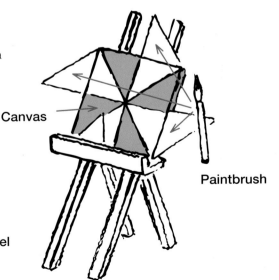

Canvas

Paintbrush

Canvas + Paintbrush = Super Pinwheel

How to Fold a Super Pinwheel

The instructions for folding a Super Pinwheel, the basic form for making cube art, follow. Steps 3 and 5 may see to be too much of a bother, but the key to folding the Super Pinwheel is making firm and accurate creases. Though it may take extra time for you to make these creases, these steps will help you smoothly fold the form in the end. You will realize the benefit of these extra folds when you start making the Pinwheel.

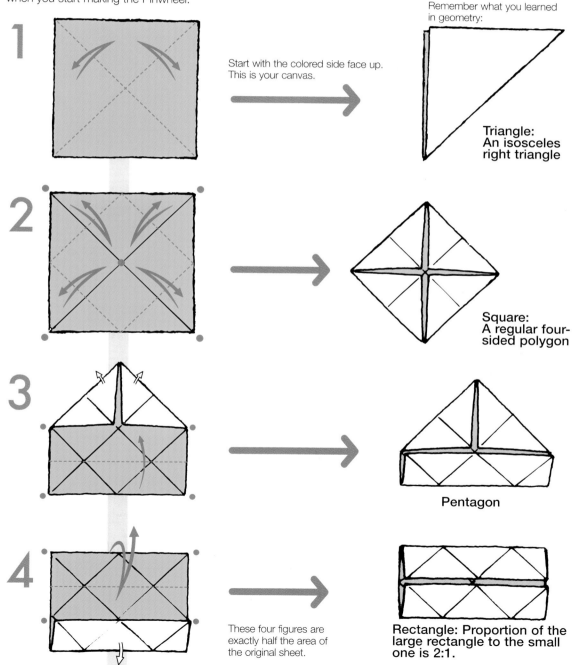

Start with the colored side face up. This is your canvas.

Remember what you learned in geometry:

Triangle:
An isosceles right triangle

Square:
A regular four-sided polygon

Pentagon

These four figures are exactly half the area of the original sheet.

Rectangle: Proportion of the large rectangle to the small one is 2:1.

Continued on the next page.

5 These folds, though seemingly unnecessary, are a technique to make useful creases that will help you fold the model faster.

Super Pinwheels

MOVIE

Completed model

Clockwise

Counterclockwise

6 Unfold.

Fold down flaps one by one, and press them firmly.

12

11 Bring the four edge midpoints and the four points of the mountain folds to the center.

7

8 Turn over and make crossing diagonal creases.

9 Fold the same way on the reverse side.

10 Pinch and make a mountain fold at each corner.

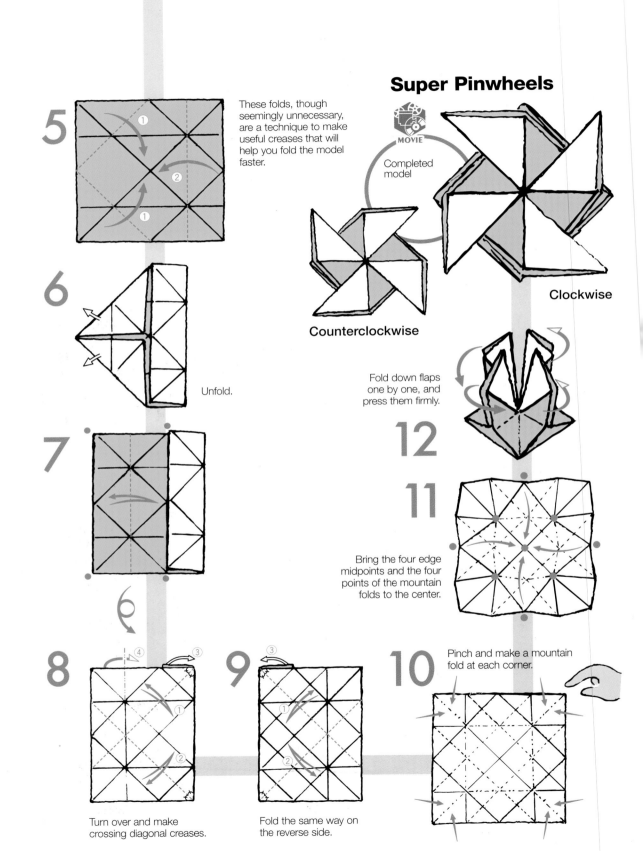

How I developed the Super Pinwheel

In Chapter 2, I described *Tamatebako* as the most intriguing origami model in *Ranma-Zushiki* and introduced a technique for assembling it, using third-fold pinwheels as modules. The Super Pinwheel came about through my exploration of techniques for making cubes, using quarter-fold pinwheels. After much trial and error—a rewarding process, in fact—I finally discovered a folding technique for the Super Pinwheel.

Cube art requires the Super Pinwheel as either the canvas or the paint-brush. Learn how to fold it from the instructions on the previous page, and make several of them before you try your hand at cube art. Have fun mastering the techniques for origami painting.

Super Pinwheel (Version 1)

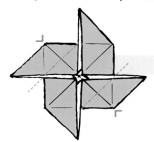
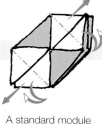

A standard module

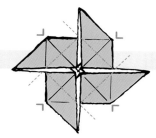

Super Pinwheel (Version 2)

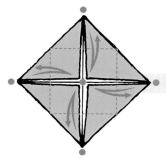
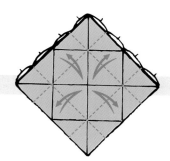

Super Pinwheel (the ultimate version)

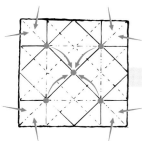

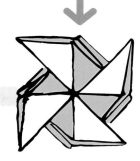

Dove of Peace

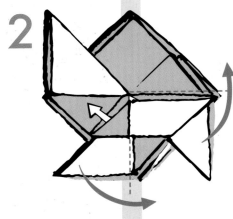

1 Fold down the upper flap (1) under the lower one (2).

2

3 Fold in numerical sequence.

4 Pull up the flap to form the dove's body.

Key Point for Making Cube Art

Cube art is a totally new origami technique, so it may take you some extra time to master. But once you have become accustomed to it, you will be able to easily paint many pictures and create your own techniques to give your paintings more detail.

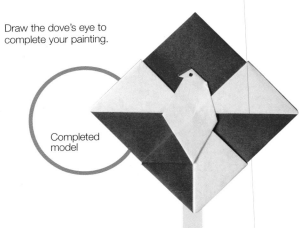

Draw the dove's eye to complete your painting.

Completed model

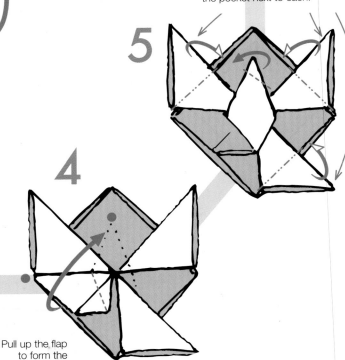

Tuck the three corners of the flaps into the pocket next to each.

5

Flying Crane

1

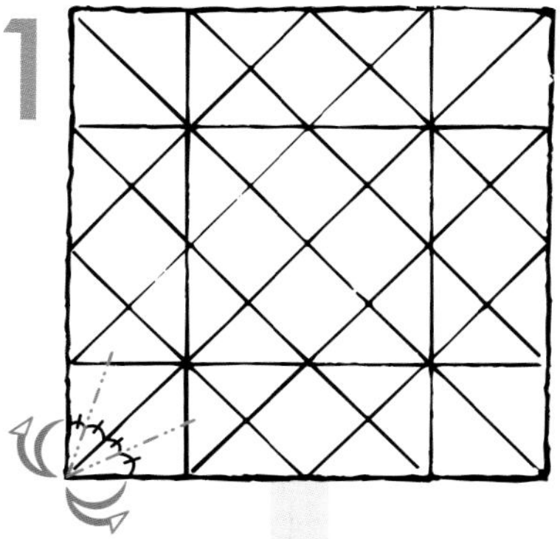

Unfold the Super Pinwheel and make a crease at the corner.

You have turned the basic crane form into more realistic image.

Completed model

Hide the corner of the wing under the crane's neck.

10 Tuck the corner into the pocket.

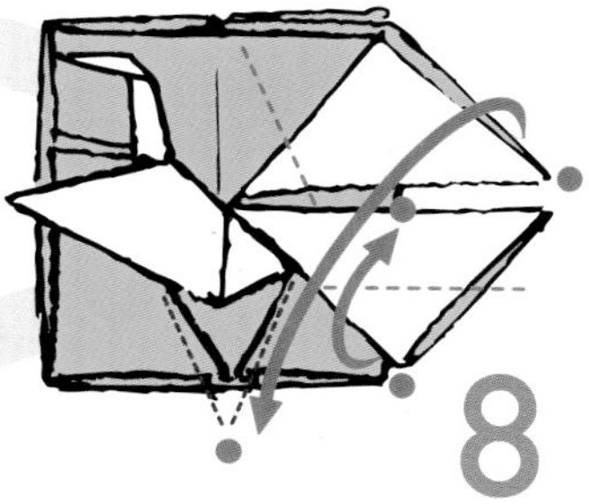

9 Tuck the corner into the pocket.

2

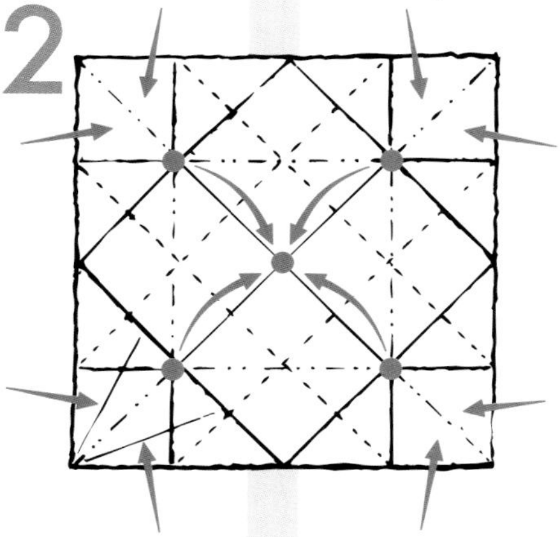

Fold the paper back into the Super Pinwheel.

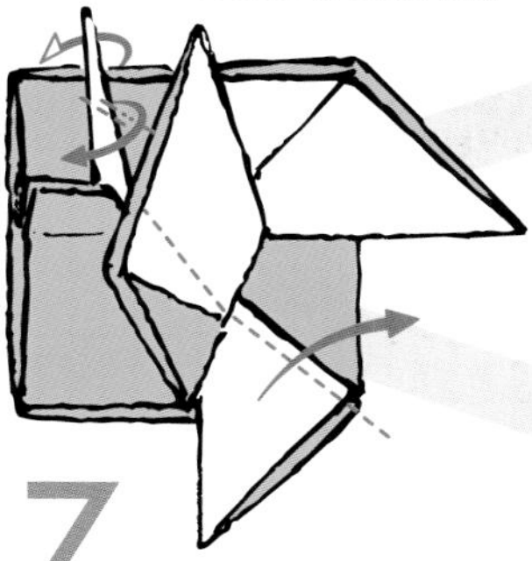

Make the crane's head with an outside reverse fold.

7

8

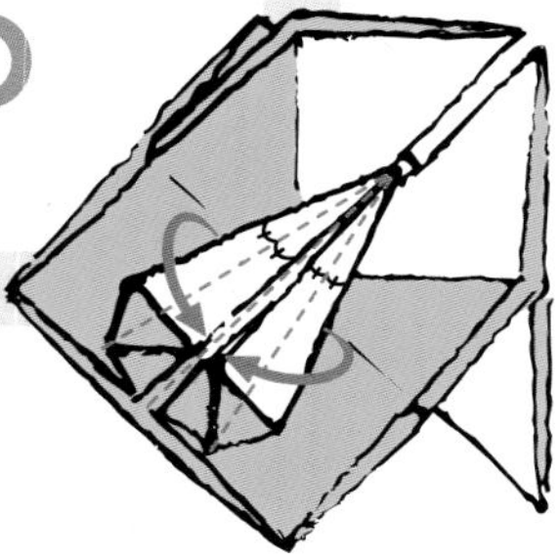

6 Make the crane's neck with an inside reverse fold.

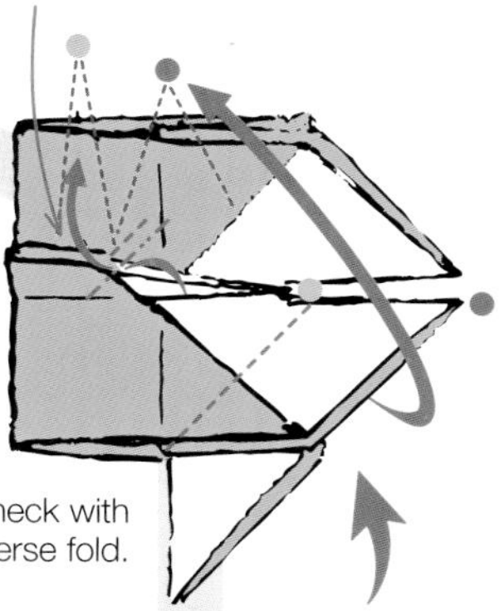

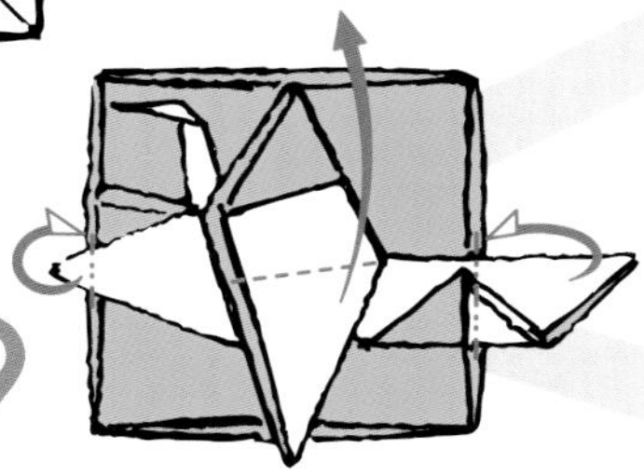

Fold down in the direction that each arrow points.

3

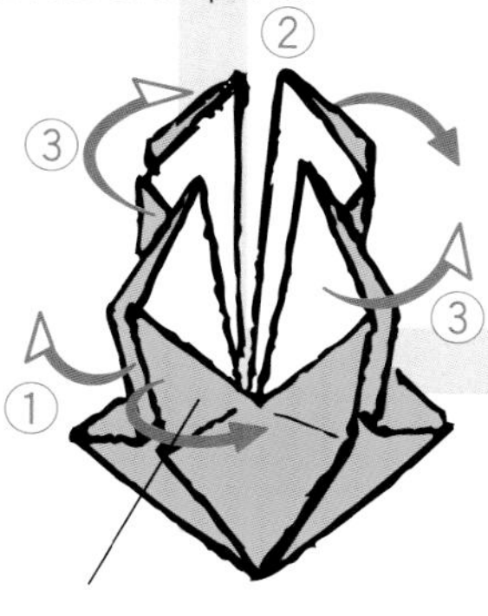

②
③
③
①

Open and fold down the flap.

4

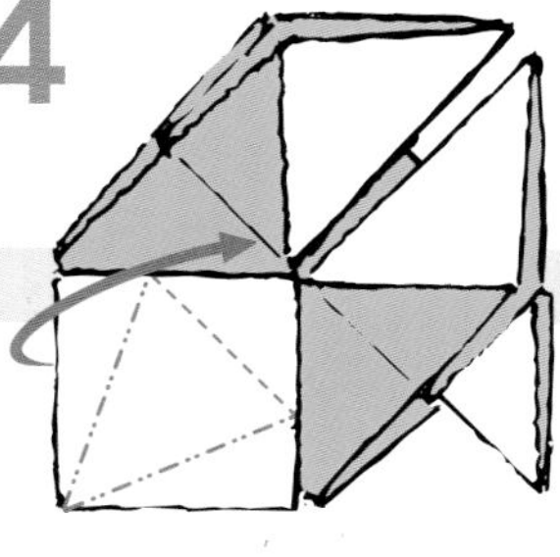

5

Eagle or Hawk

1

Fold in numerical sequence.

② ①

Open the flap.

Draw a sharp eye to make it look real.

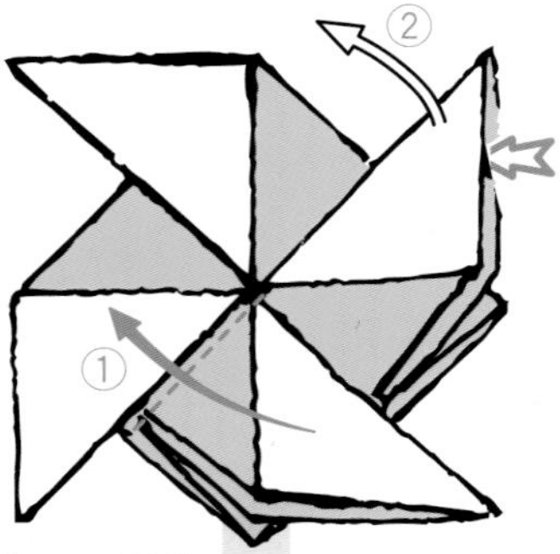

Completed model

How to Fold the Head

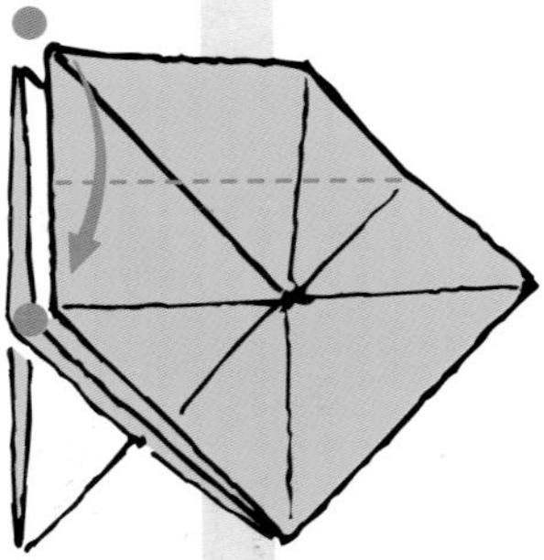

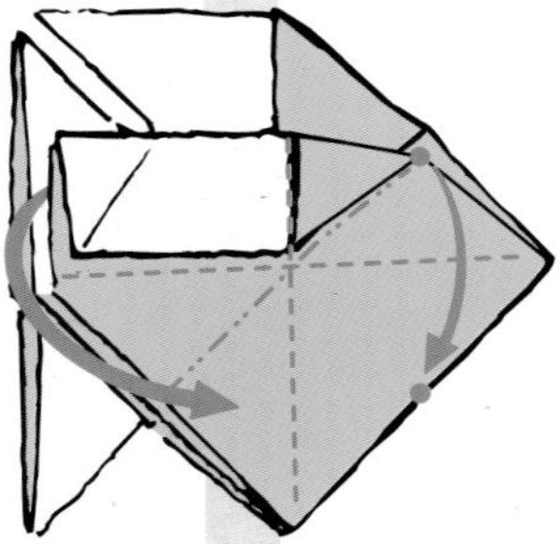

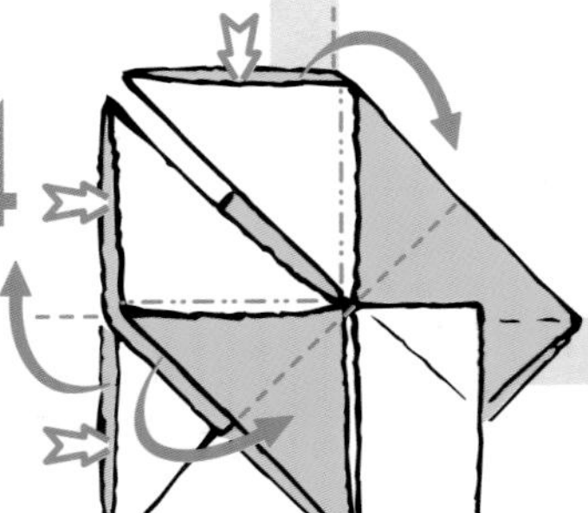

2 •
•

8
Tuck the three corners into the pockets next to each.

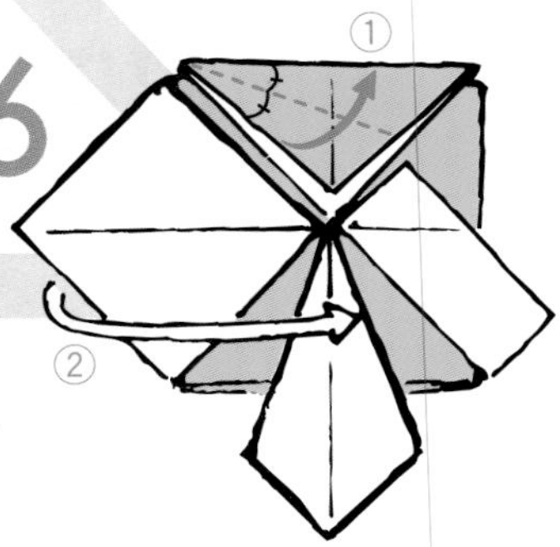

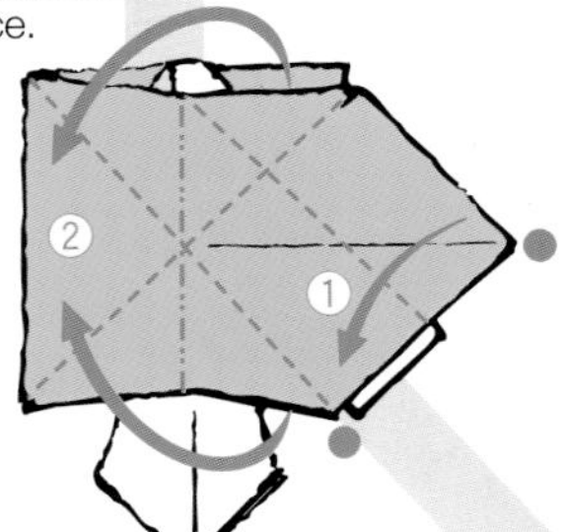

Open the flap as you tilt it to the left.

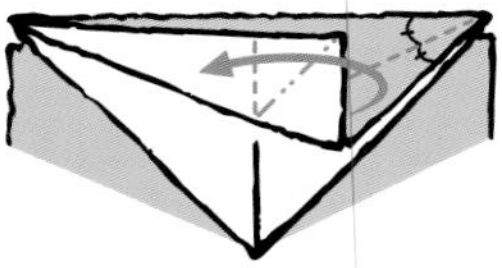

Fold in every point to make a beak.

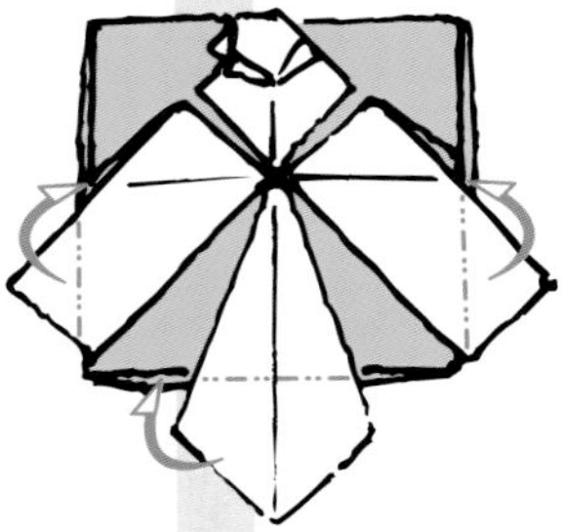

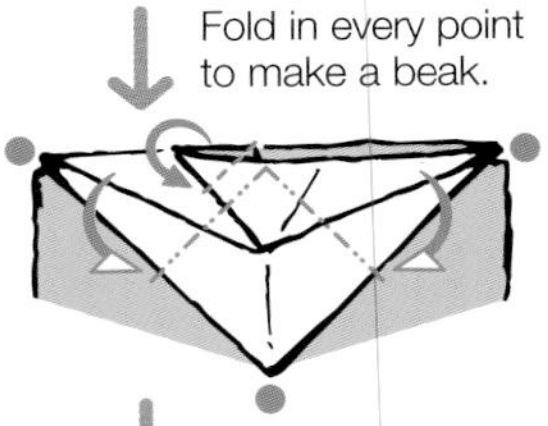

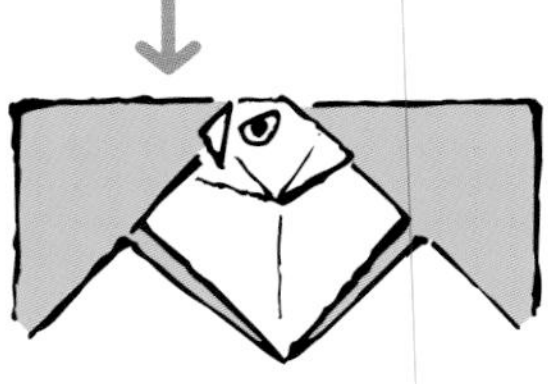

3

7
Fold in numerical sequence.
② ①
•
•
•

Draw an eye.

4

5

6
Fold the head before you go to the next step.
①
②

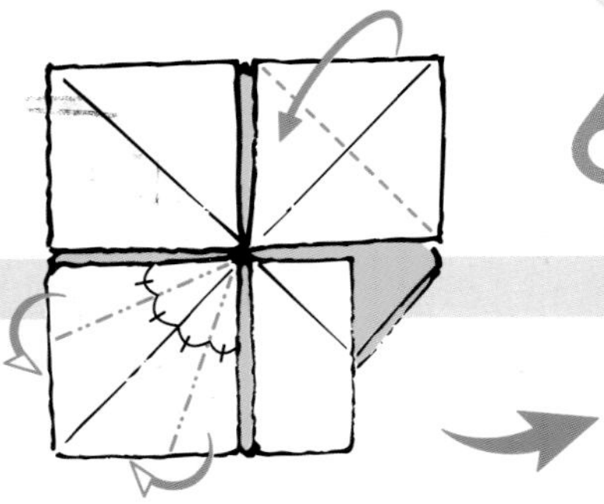

Owl

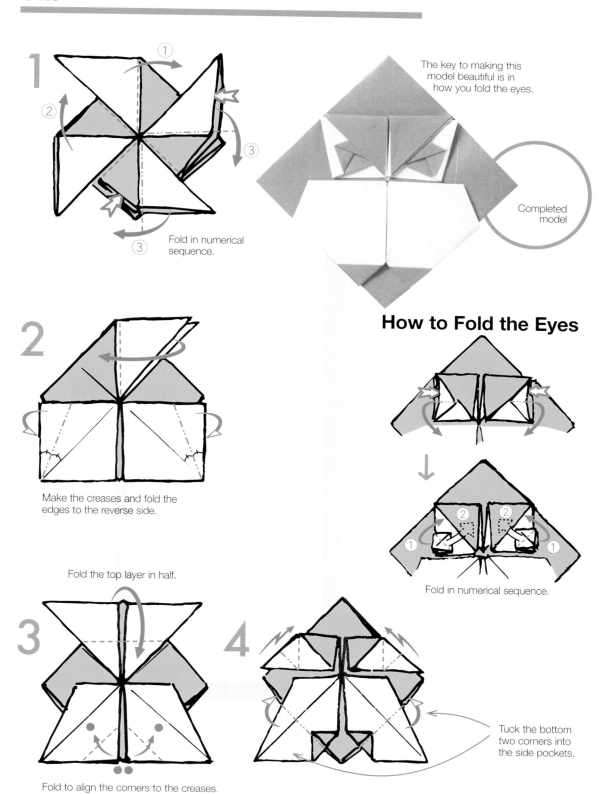

1

① ② ③

③ Fold in numerical sequence.

The key to making this model beautiful is in how you fold the eyes.

Completed model

2

Make the creases and fold the edges to the reverse side.

How to Fold the Eyes

① ② ② ①

Fold in numerical sequence.

3

Fold the top layer in half.

Fold to align the corners to the creases.

4

Tuck the bottom two corners into the side pockets.

Lovebird

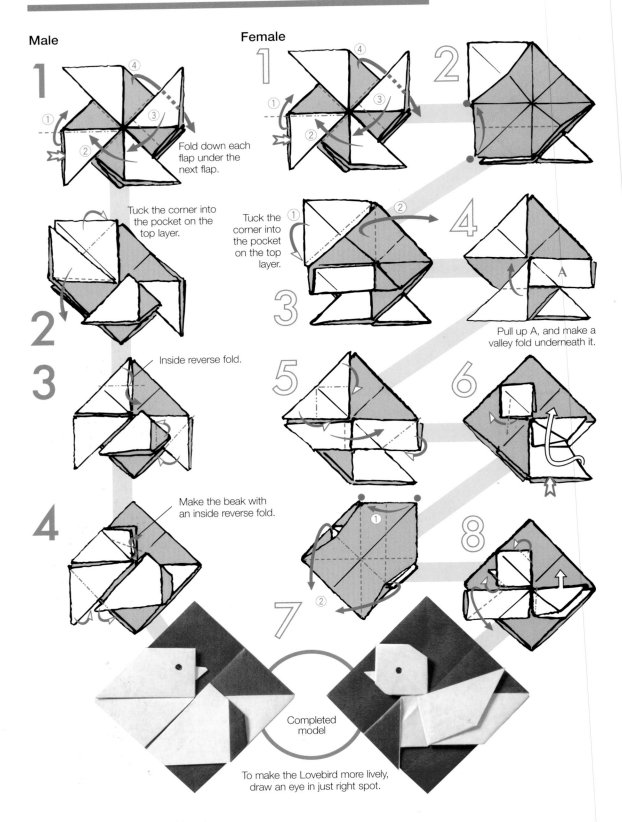

Male

1 Fold down each flap under the next flap.

2 Tuck the corner into the pocket on the top layer.

3 Inside reverse fold.

4 Make the beak with an inside reverse fold.

Female

1

2

3 Tuck the corner into the pocket on the top layer.

4 Pull up A, and make a valley fold underneath it.

5

6

7

8

Completed model

To make the Lovebird more lively, draw an eye in just right spot.

Mermaid

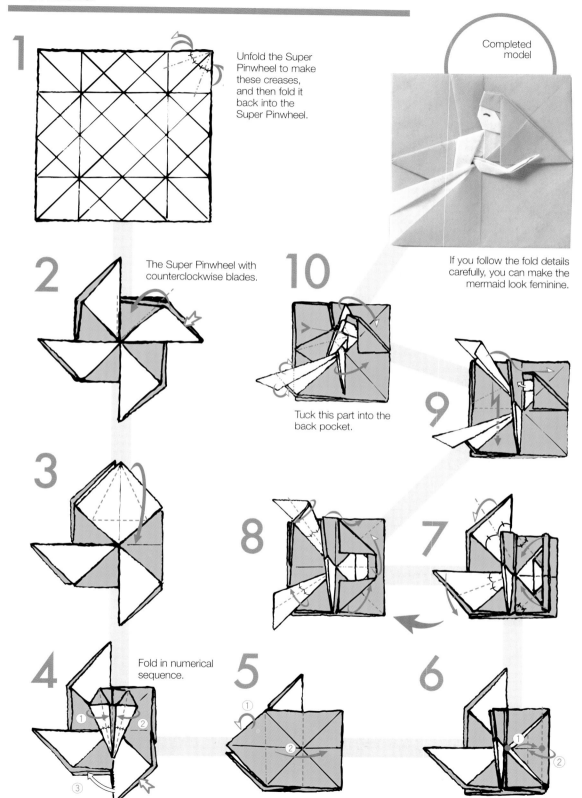

1 Unfold the Super Pinwheel to make these creases, and then fold it back into the Super Pinwheel.

Completed model

If you follow the fold details carefully, you can make the mermaid look feminine.

2 The Super Pinwheel with counterclockwise blades.

3

4 Fold in numerical sequence.

5

6

7

8

9

10 Tuck this part into the back pocket.

Dolphin

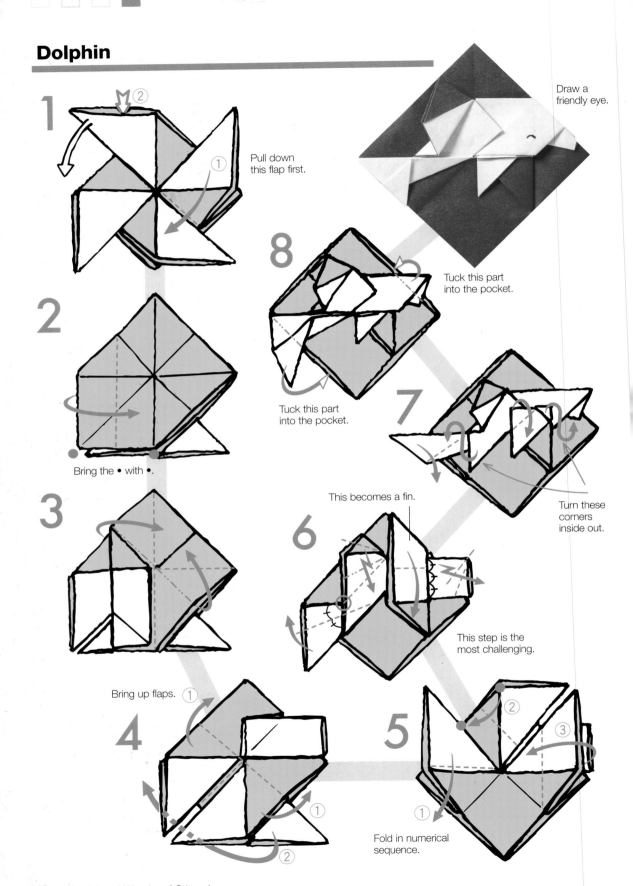

1 Pull down this flap first.

Draw a friendly eye.

2 Bring the • with •.

3

4 Bring up flaps.

5 Fold in numerical sequence.

6 This becomes a fin.

This step is the most challenging.

7 Turn these corners inside out.

8 Tuck this part into the pocket.

Tuck this part into the pocket.

Cube Art-Oriental Zodiac Animals

Rat

1 ① Counterclockwise ③ ②

Completed model

Fold only the flap into the pocket.

2

Your final challenge is to make the rat look appealing.

Turn these corners inside out.

5

Make a leg by folding at ○.

The flap in the pocket when folded.

3

4

This is the rat's tail.

Ox

1 Fold down. ① ③ ②

To the reverse side

2

3

Fold in half.

Be careful—this part is folded too tight to be opened easily.

Fold over this part, and position it on the center horizontal axis.

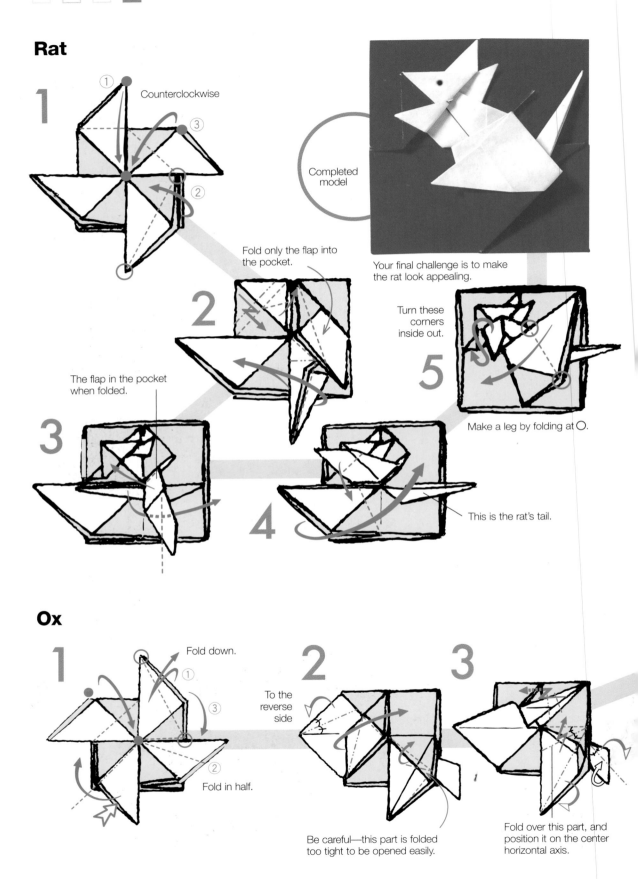

Tiger

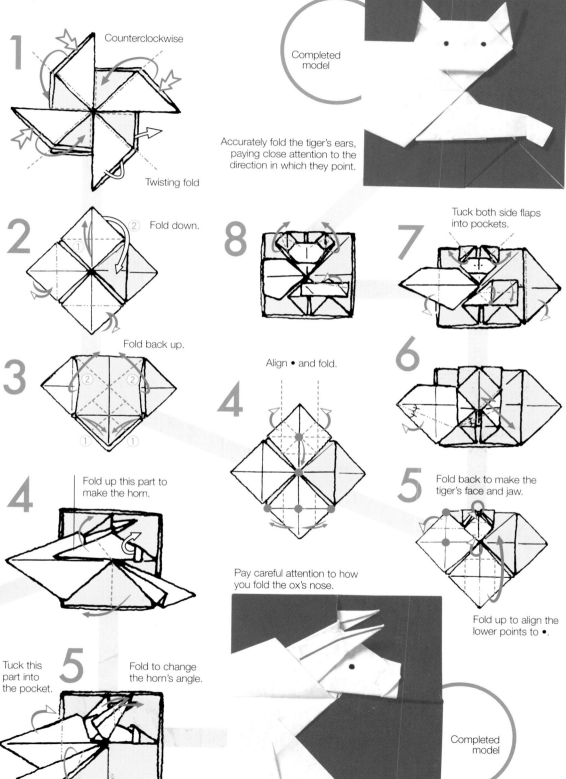

1 Counterclockwise

Twisting fold

Completed model

Accurately fold the tiger's ears, paying close attention to the direction in which they point.

2 ② Fold down.

Fold back up.

3

8

7 Tuck both side flaps into pockets.

Align • and fold.

4

6

4 Fold up this part to make the horn.

5 Fold back to make the tiger's face and jaw.

Pay careful attention to how you fold the ox's nose.

Fold up to align the lower points to •.

Completed model

5 Tuck this part into the pocket.

Fold to change the horn's angle.

Rabbit

1

Open the flap to reveal the colored side.

Counterclockwise

① ②

Open the flap to reveal the white side.

You can draw the eye using this picture as a guide.

Completed model

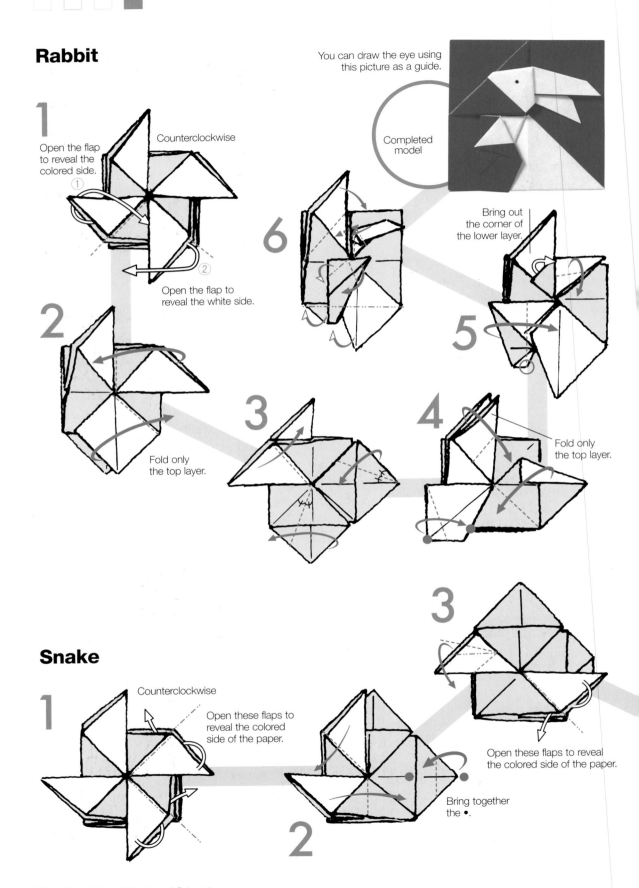

2

Fold only the top layer.

3

4

Fold only the top layer.

5

Bring out the corner of the lower layer.

6

Snake

1

Counterclockwise

Open these flaps to reveal the colored side of the paper.

2

Bring together the •.

3

Open these flaps to reveal the colored side of the paper.

Dragon

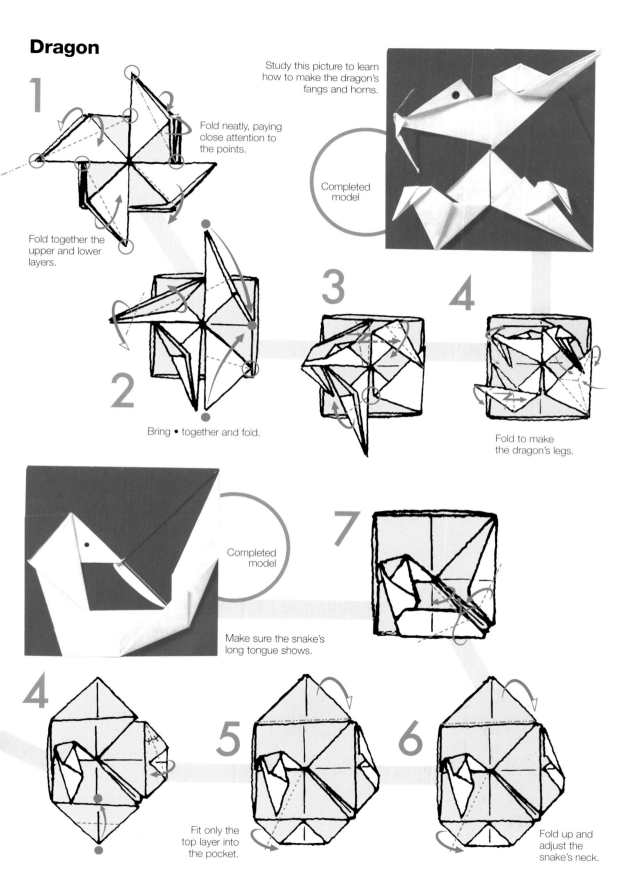

1

Fold neatly, paying close attention to the points.

Fold together the upper and lower layers.

Study this picture to learn how to make the dragon's fangs and horns.

Completed model

2

Bring • together and fold.

3

4

Fold to make the dragon's legs.

Completed model

Make sure the snake's long tongue shows.

7

4

5

Fit only the top layer into the pocket.

6

Fold up and adjust the snake's neck.

Horse

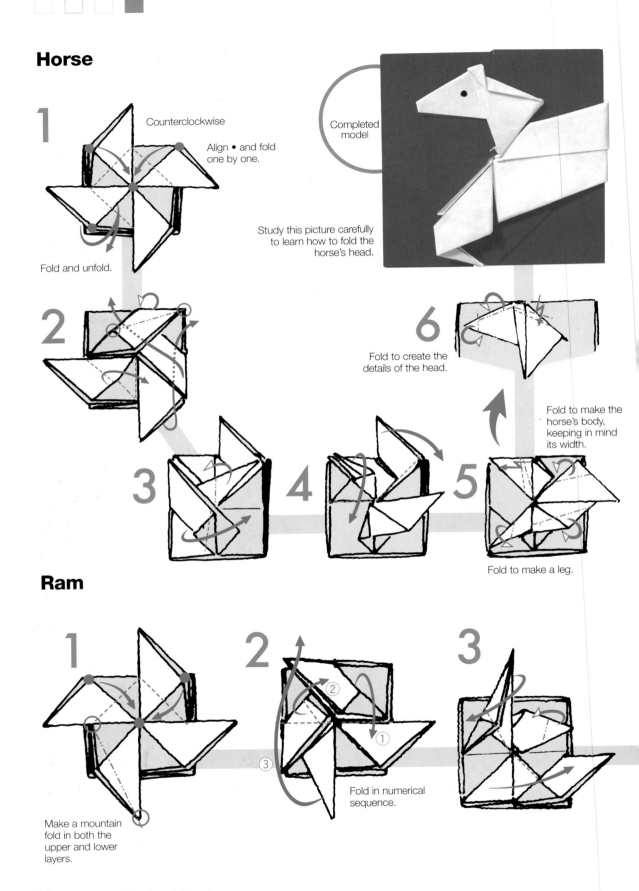

1 Counterclockwise

Align • and fold one by one.

Fold and unfold.

Completed model

Study this picture carefully to learn how to fold the horse's head.

2

3

4

5 Fold to make a leg.

Fold to make the horse's body, keeping in mind its width.

6 Fold to create the details of the head.

Ram

1 Make a mountain fold in both the upper and lower layers.

2 Fold in numerical sequence.

3

Monkey

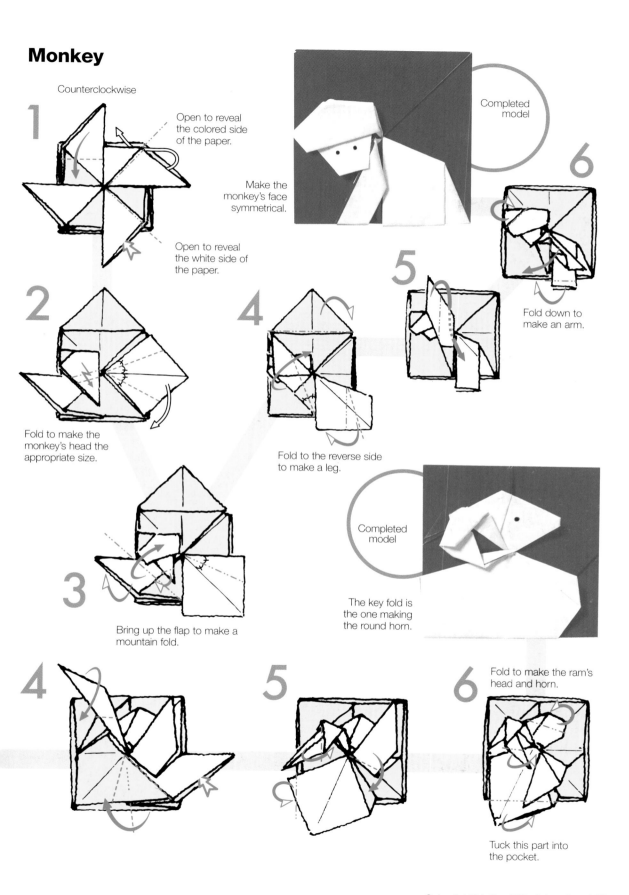

Counterclockwise

1

Open to reveal the colored side of the paper.

Make the monkey's face symmetrical.

Open to reveal the white side of the paper.

Completed model

2

Fold to make the monkey's head the appropriate size.

3

Bring up the flap to make a mountain fold.

4

Fold to the reverse side to make a leg.

5

6

Fold down to make an arm.

Completed model

The key fold is the one making the round horn.

4

5

6

Fold to make the ram's head and horn.

Tuck this part into the pocket.

Rooster

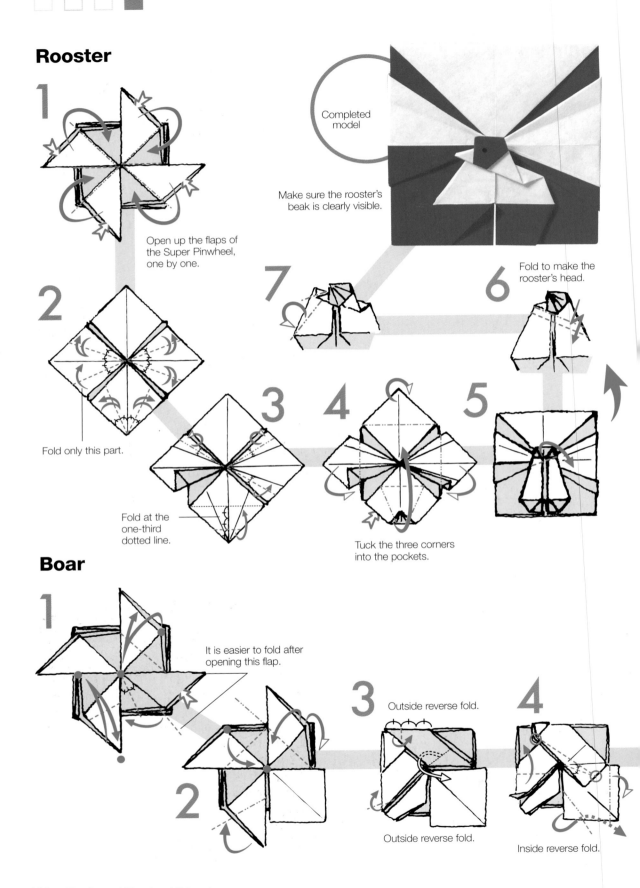

1 Open up the flaps of the Super Pinwheel, one by one.

Completed model

Make sure the rooster's beak is clearly visible.

2 Fold only this part.

3 Fold at the one-third dotted line.

4 Tuck the three corners into the pockets.

5

6 Fold to make the rooster's head.

7

Boar

1 It is easier to fold after opening this flap.

2

3 Outside reverse fold.

Outside reverse fold.

4 Inside reverse fold.

Dog

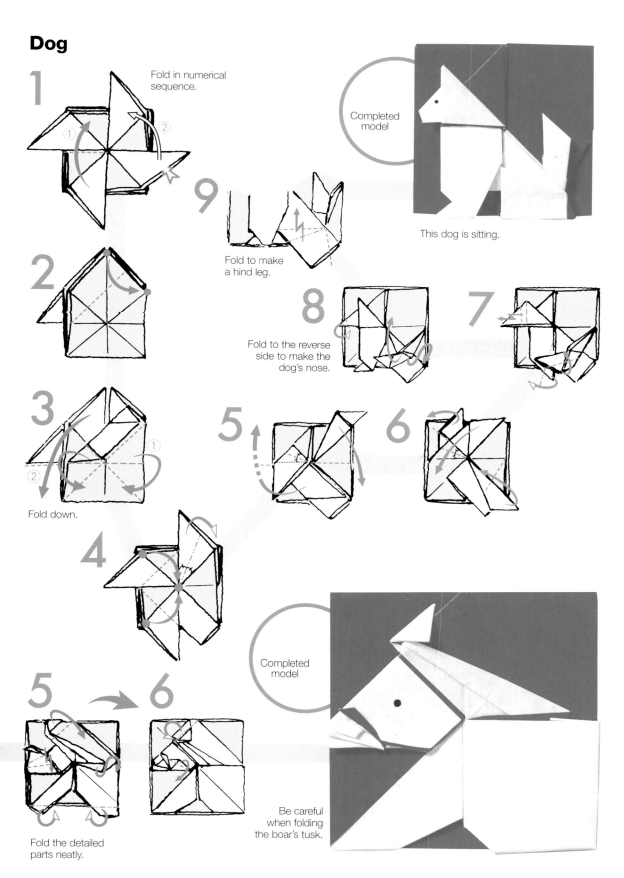

1 Fold in numerical sequence.

2

3 Fold down.

4

5 → **6** Fold the detailed parts neatly.

9 Fold to make a hind leg.

8 Fold to the reverse side to make the dog's nose.

7

5

6

Completed model

This dog is sitting.

Completed model

Be careful when folding the boar's tusk.

Solutions

The solutions to the questions posed in the section, "Puzzles Based on Traditional Models," are shown on pages 122–124.

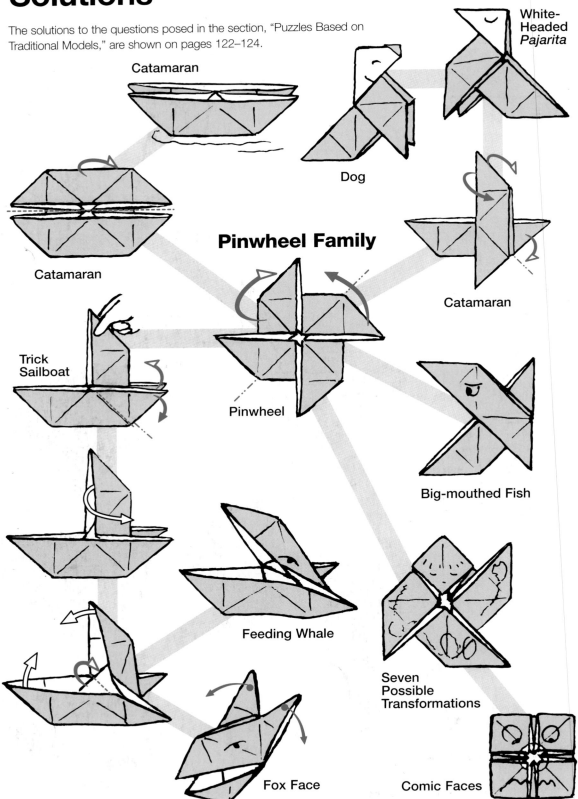

Catamaran

White-Headed *Pajarita*

Dog

Catamaran

Pinwheel Family

Catamaran

Trick Sailboat

Pinwheel

Big-mouthed Fish

Feeding Whale

Seven Possible Transformations

Fox Face

Comic Faces

Yakko Family

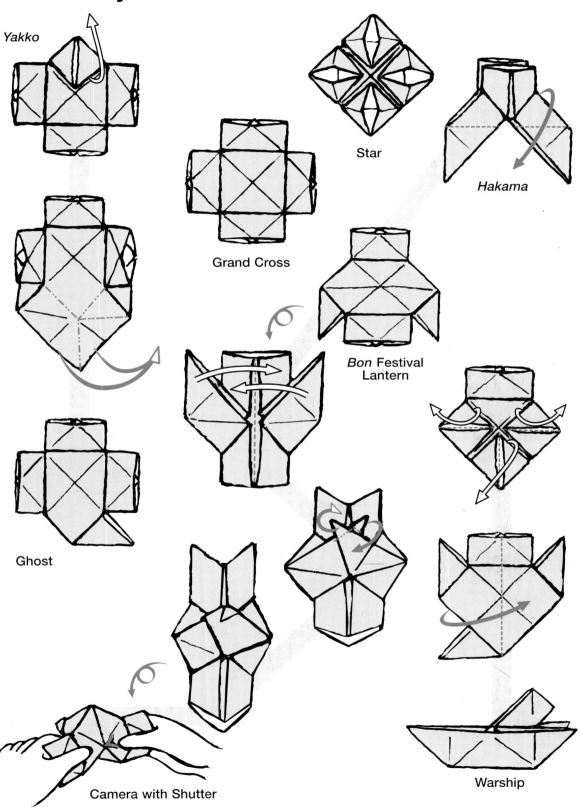

Yakko

Star

Hakama

Grand Cross

Bon Festival
Lantern

Ghost

Camera with Shutter

Warship

Yakko Family

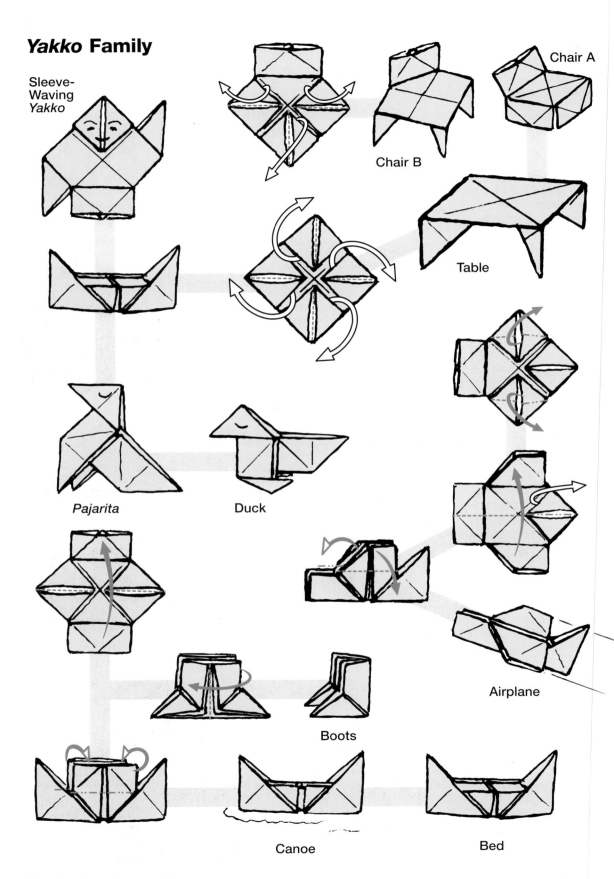

Sleeve-
Waving
Yakko

Chair A

Chair B

Table

Pajarita

Duck

Airplane

Boots

Canoe

Bed

The answers to the questions in the section called "Partial Inversion Puzzles," are found on pages 125–134.

Boat with a White Sail

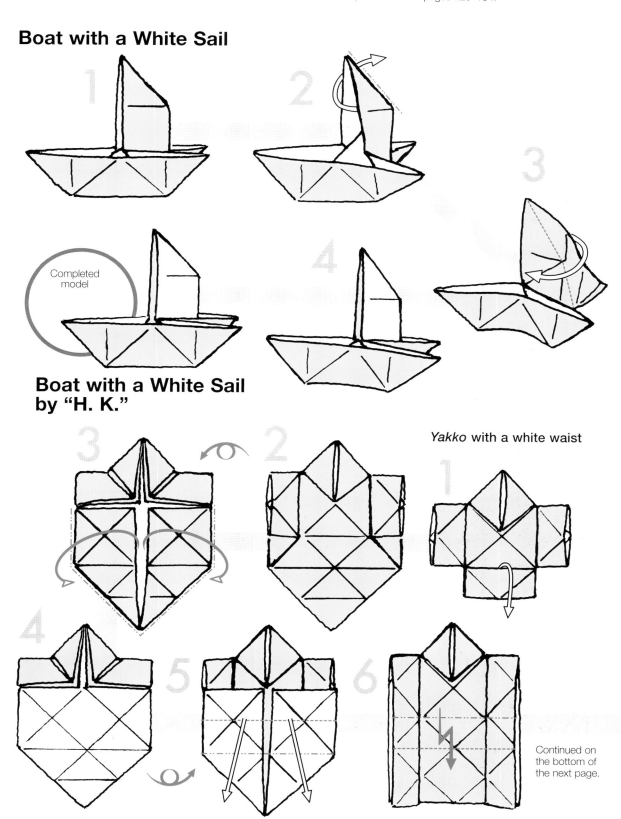

Completed model

Boat with a White Sail by "H. K."

Yakko with a white waist

Continued on the bottom of the next page.

Hakama with a White Waistband

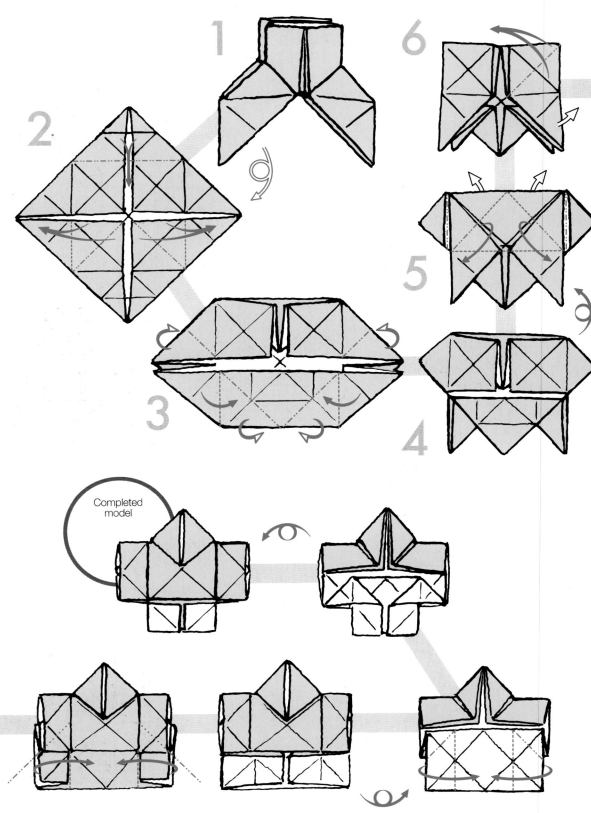

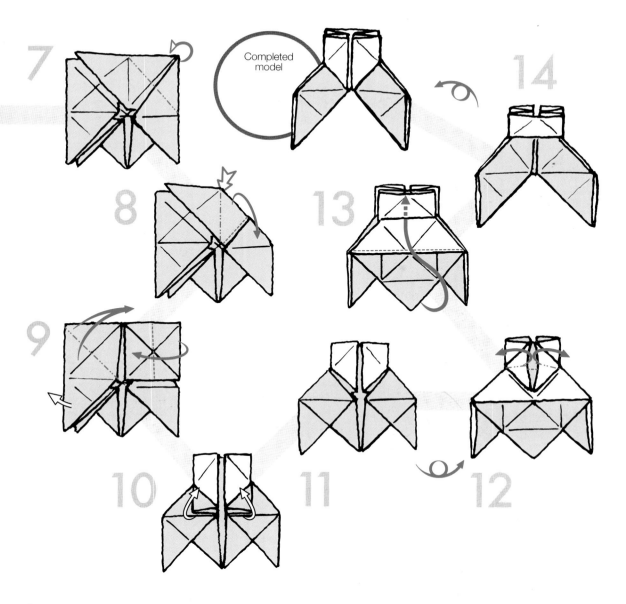

Completed model

Sleeve-Waving *Yakko* with a White Face

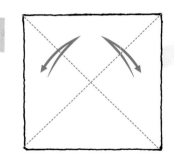

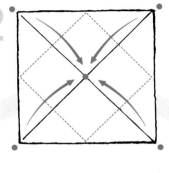

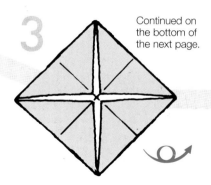

Continued on the bottom of the next page.

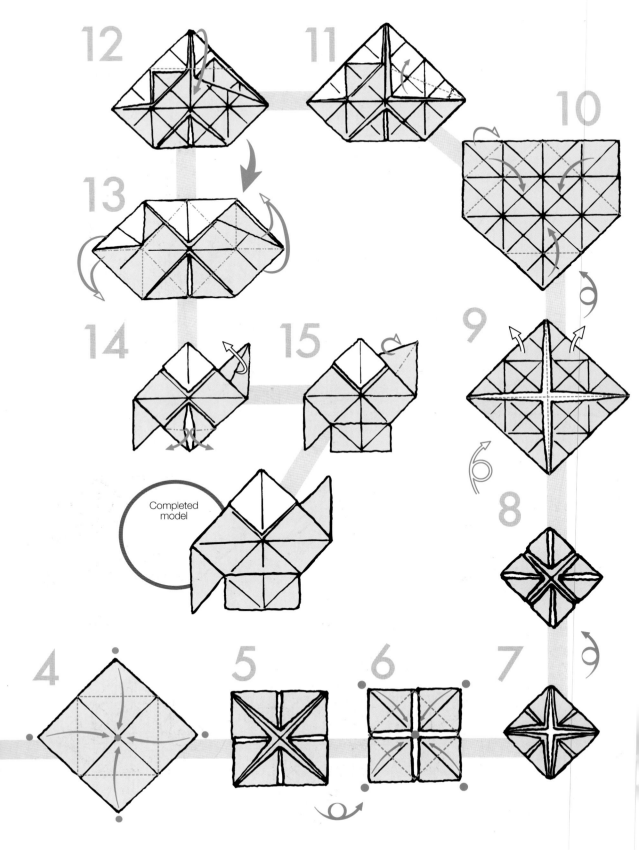

Completed
model

Rider and His Legs

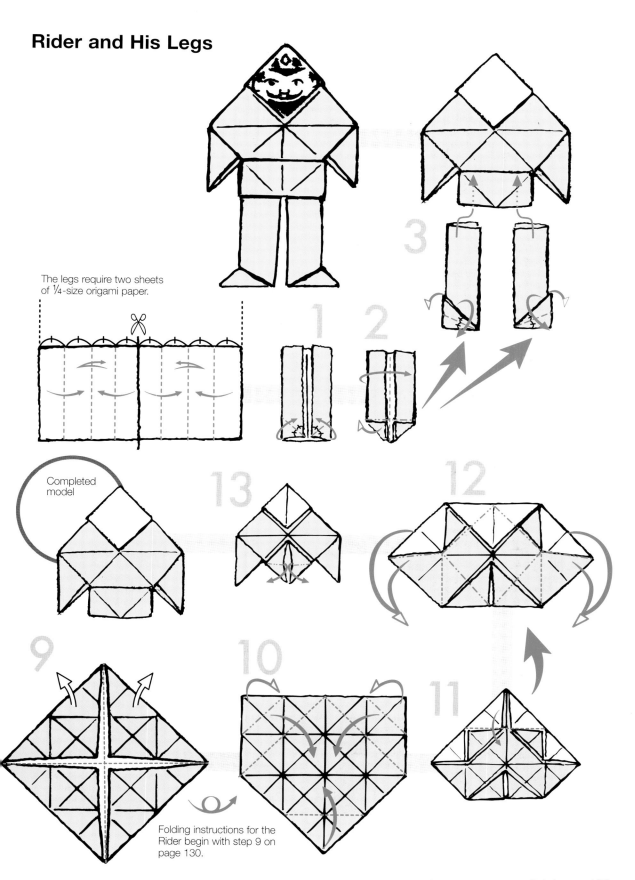

The legs require two sheets of ¼-size origami paper.

3

1   2

Completed model

13

12

9

10

11

Folding instructions for the Rider begin with step 9 on page 130.

Rider and His Legs (continued)

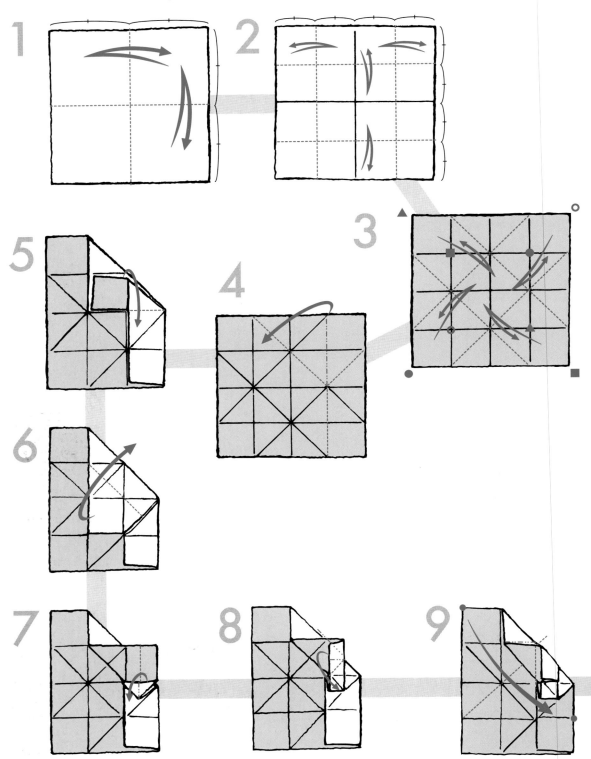

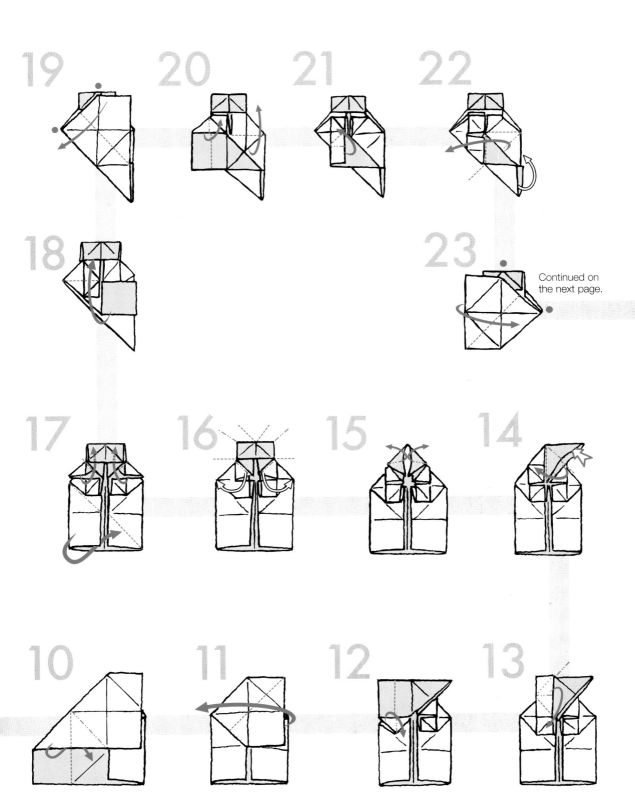

Continued on the next page.

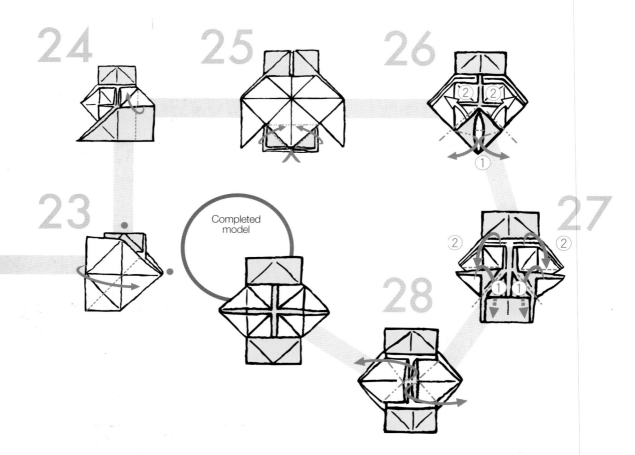

24 **25** **26**

23

Completed
model

27

28

Bon Festival Lantern with a White Body

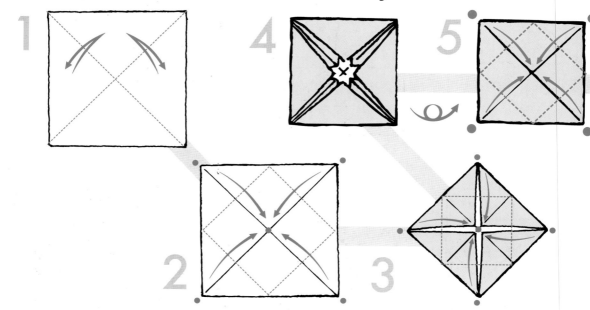

1

4

5

2

3

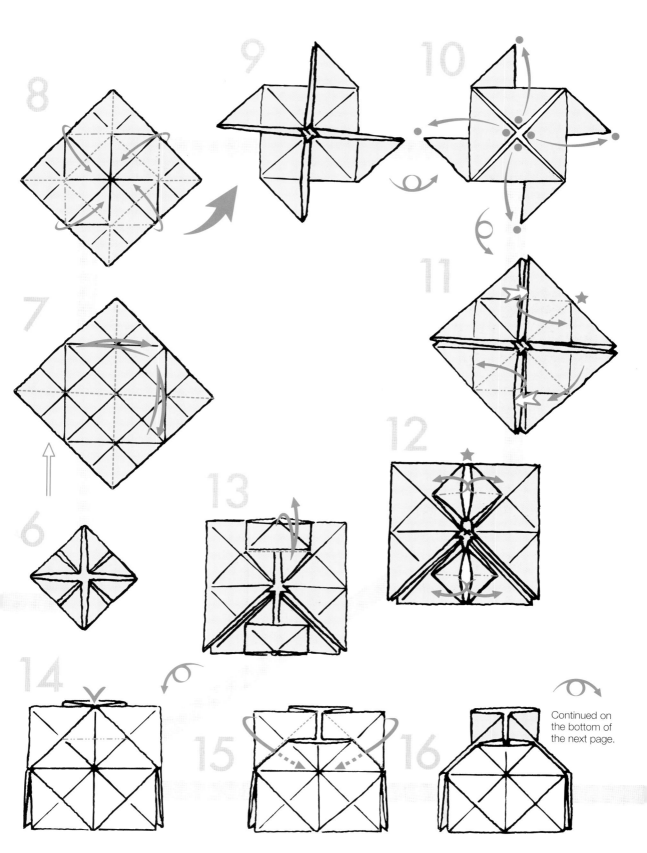

Continued on
the bottom of
the next page.

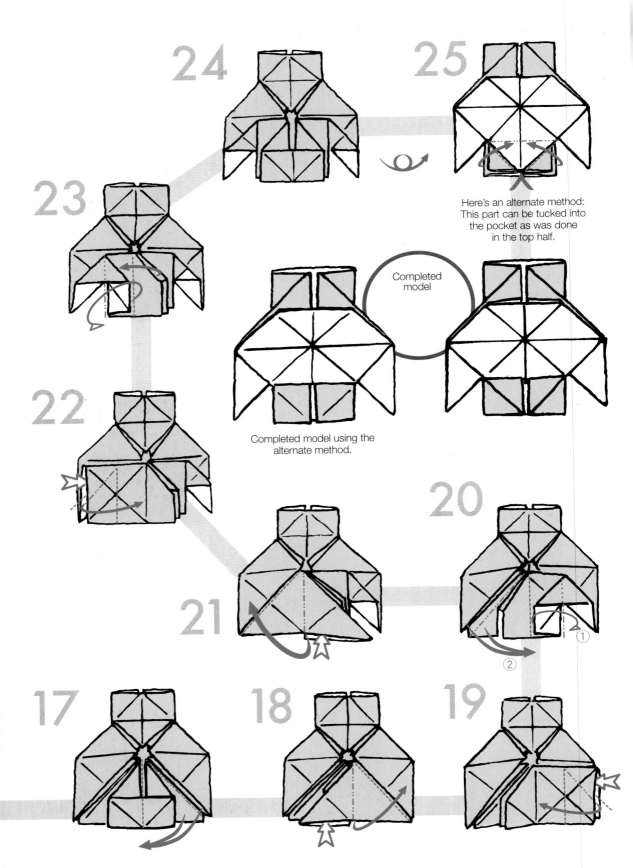

24

25

Here's an alternate method:
This part can be tucked into
the pocket as was done
in the top half.

23

Completed
model

22

Completed model using the
alternate method.

21

20

①

②

17

18

19

About the Origami Data Collections on the CD-ROM

The CD-ROM included with this book contains two collections of origami data, Original *Chiyogami* Design Collection and Crease-lined Origami Data Collection. All files are in PDF format.

In the PDF folder

chiyogami

This folder contains the Original *Chiyogami* Design Collection.

orisen_data

This folder contains the Crease-lined *Origami* Data Collection.

How to Use the Data

Original *Chiyogami* Design Collection

Each file contains 10 types of *chiyogami* pattern designs. Open a file for any pattern you like (see the filename) using Acrobat Reader, and print it to use for folding your origami models.

Crease-lined Origami Data Collection

This folder contains 13 crease-lined origami model sheets. Open a file for any work of your choice (see the filename) using Acrobat Reader, and print it to use for folding a model. When you need to check or print all the origami works at once, use the file orisen_data_all.

The CD-ROM also contains an Adobe Acrobat Reader Installer, in case your computer does not have Acrobat Reader.

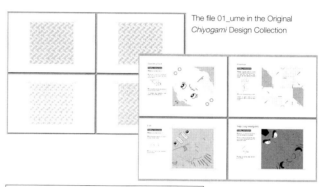

The file 01_ume in the Original *Chiyogami* Design Collection

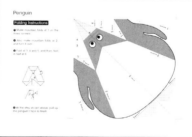

The file orisen_data_all in the Crease-lined Origami Data Collection

After you print an origami data sheet, cut out the marked square along the line on the printed sheet. The square is the same size as standard origami paper.

About the Author

Modern origami pioneer Kunihiko Kasahara was born in Okaya City, Nagano, Japan in 1941. He studied broadcasting at Nihon University's College of Art, where his interest in origami began. Over the years, he developed new techniques in origami art and wrote about them in several books, which have been translated into English, German, and Korean. His first publication, *Origami Book for Mother and Child* (Seiko-sha, 1965), was displayed at the Japanese pavilion of the Osaka Expo in 1970, and was later packed into a time capsule that will be sealed for 5,000 years. In 1986, he taught in Brazil and Chili as a Japan Foundation lecturer and has been active in various international cultural exchanges. He is known as the pioneer of the innovative "unit-origami" technique. His latest achievement, the "cube art" introduced in this book, is designed to reveal the artistic beauty in geometric figures. It's a style that no other origami artist had previously attempted. He currently lives in Kanagawa, Japan.